# THERE'S MORE

Infinite Blessings for the Spirit-Filled Life
by
Robert Benjamin Hall

Logos International
Plainfield, N.J.

# TABLE OF CONTENTS

# CHAPTER ONE

## THE FRUITS OF THE SPIRIT

A story is told of sailors who were dying of thirst after a long voyage to South America. They had nearly reached the land—they knew it was just over the horizon—but they were doomed because their water supplies were exhausted. At the last possible moment before they expired, another boat appeared and as it drew near, hailed them and asked if there was anything they needed. The dying crew cried, "Water, water." The other sailors pointed to the sea all around them and made signs to indicate that they could drink it. Their vessel had reached the outpouring of the mighty Amazon River, which carries its fresh water many, many miles out to sea.

There are church members today who are dying of thirst in the midst of fountains of living water because they do not know what is available. Or to change the metaphor slightly, there are Christians today who are being fed just enough to keep them alive, but who are suffering from spiritual malnutrition because they are not receiving enough of the tremendous variety of food which God offers their starving spirits. The message of this book is that be you neophyte or saint, there's more.

A young priest of the Episcopal Church came to me for counseling one day. He had just celebrated the tenth anniversary of his ordination. In worldly terms, his ministry was a success; he had a large and growing church in a fashionable suburb of a lovely city. But his life was empty. "Bob," he said, "if I thought the next ten years were going to be like the last ten, I'd leave the ministry."

Yes, there's more to come. Not just more of the same, not just the same old days following after one another in the same tired old pattern; no, there's more than this in store for you. God has promised us abundant life; there's more of this abundance than any of us has yet seen. God has promised us the victory through Jesus Christ; there are yet many victories to be won. Yes, my friends, there's more.

If you are completely and totally satisfied in every realm of your life, there's no point in reading further, because what we have to say will be of no interest to you. But if you are disappointed in what life has given you, if you have problems that you can't surmount, if the world seems to be passing you by, or if you are doing pretty well, but know you could be doing better, take hope—there's more to come.

The old sideshow barker used to urge people to buy their tickets and come on to the inside. "Folks," he'd say, "you ain't seen nothin' yet." So come along to the inside with me, and let's see what God has in store for you. Let's see how God can make a successful life out of a sad one, an extraordinary life out of one that's just run-of-the-mill.

You know that we live in many different circles, some of which intersect, and some of which are quite separate from the others. Take stock now . . .

How are things at home?
How are things at work?
How are you doing in your church?
How are things in your playtime?
How are things at school?
How are you serving your community?

If you find a lack in any one of these areas of life, if things are not going well, if something needs changing, persevere; things need not continue as they are. Today is not the end, there's more.

I remember a retired schoolteacher in my first parish who greeted my initial attempts to teach the Christian faith with a rejection that I found very frustrating. She asserted very confidently, "I have been the kind of person that I am for many, many years, and I certainly haven't come to church to be changed." How often those of us who say in the ritual, "As it was in the beginning, is now and ever shall be, world without end," are freezing our religious development at a very low level.

If you have tried Christianity and found it wanting, consider whether or not you have tried a child's Christianity. Ask yourself if it is not possible that what you have rejected was only an imperfect understanding of only a tiny part of the truth. Consider that your whole attitude toward religion might be different if you found out, as others have, that—there's more.

Just as God has for each of us a thousand tomorrows all bright and new, so He has a thousand pathways about which we have never thought, let alone traveled. Some of these pathways are uniquely reserved for you; they are precise answers to your special need. Other pathways are already known to many, and you can have company along the way.

Your journey through life need not be stalled nor stagnant, wherever you may be; there is another step just waiting to be taken. Your life is unique; there is no other quite like it among the billions on earth, but wherever your life has led you at this moment of time, something wonderful and new is waiting for you if you will but let go and let God. A radiant Christian named Frances Gardner was speaking at our church one night when she sounded the keynote for this. "I wake up every morning," she bubbled, "asking God what fabulous thing He's going to do today."

When Jesus took leave of His disciples after teaching them for three years and after they had seen the crucifixion and the resurrection and had had forty days of postgraduate training with Him, He said, "I have yet many things to say to you but you cannot bear them now. Howbeit when He, the Spirit of truth is come, He will teach you all things." Few of us can claim to know as much as the disciples did, and they had more to learn when the Holy Spirit came. The Holy Spirit still comes, into your life and mine, and He teaches and empowers and brings gifts and fruits and evidences of God's love for us. We have much to learn, too. That is what this book is all about. It is not an exhaustive list of all the things that God does, but it may hint to you that there's more to come.

There begins to be more for you as soon as you begin to walk in the Spirit. Notice the capital "S." This is not your spirit but the Holy Spirit of God. It is possible to be possessed by this Spirit, to have your life so filled with Him that you no longer live but Christ liveth in you. That might sound a little corny to start off with, but you will see that life in the Spirit carries with it a freedom and a joy that marks the beginning of the abundant life we are talking about.

When the power of the Spirit came upon the disciples at Pentecost and they began to preach and teach, the change in their lives was so marked that people listened with awe. Peter stood up and told about Jesus and what God was doing in the world through Him. And when he paused for breath, someone called out to Peter and the rest of the apostles, "Men and brethren, what shall we do?" Peter's reply is relevant to us today. He said, "Repent and be baptized every one of you in the name of Jesus Christ for the remission of sins, and you shall receive the gift of the Holy Spirit."

Many have been baptized without repentance; many have gone through the forms of church ceremonies either as children or as basically uninvolved adults and have not received the gift of the Holy Spirit that God offers. It is because this is so widely true that we can say, "There's more." For when you open your life to the indwelling of that Spirit, when you are ready to receive what God has already given, then a whole new realm opens up to you. This is the abundant life we are promised.

In these pages we are going to talk about the gifts of the Spirit which are manifested in the life of a Spirit-filled Christian as God's power comes upon him. We will describe some of the marks or evidences of a Spirit-filled life as we have seen them in the changed life-style of present-day Christians. We're going to begin with a description of the fruits of the Spirit, which are those character-expanding manifestations of God's presence in human life.

St. Paul says in Gal. 5:16, "Walk by the Spirit, and do not gratify the desires of the flesh." Some people think that refusing to gratify the desires of the flesh is what religion is all about. There's a story about a native chieftain who was being urged to become a Christian in his latter years, to make his peace with God before he died. And he said, "Let me understand clearly what is being asked of me. If I become a

Christian, I can no longer kill my enemies, right?" The answer was yes. "And if I become a Christian, I can no longer steal things from those weaker than myself, right?" The answer was yes. "And if I become a Christian I can no longer take any of the young girls of the village to my bed, right?" The answer was yes. The old chief shook his head in puzzlement. "To be Christian," he said, "and to be old—it is the same thing."

Well, it is true that the desires of the flesh become somewhat less pressing as one becomes older. But this is not what Christianity is all about. Jesus said, "Seek ye first the kingdom, and all these things will be added unto you." Those who walk in the Spirit find that their fleshly needs are taken care of even more abundantly than before. But their attention is focused on the things of the Spirit. The King James Version of the Bible translates this passage, "lusts of the flesh," which puts the thing in better proportion. God gave us our desires. When we put the flesh ahead of the Spirit, these desires become lusts.

In the same passage, Paul contrasts the works of the flesh with the fruit of the Spirit. The works of the flesh are immorality, impurity, licentiousness, idolatry, sorcery, enmity, strife, jealousy, anger, selfishness, dissension, party spirit, envy, drunkenness, and carousing. These are obviously the result of giving way to the desires of the flesh and letting them gain the ascendancy.

But the fruit of the Spirit, Paul says, is love, joy, peace, patience, kindness, goodness, faithfulness, gentleness, and self-control. We are going to look at each one of these individually to help us better understand how life in the Spirit brings abundance. Every one of these fruits of the Spirit is meant for every Christian and will appear one by one in a life yielded to the Spirit of Christ.

Life in the Spirit begins when you turn your life entirely over to God. By giving up everything, you gain everything. This is the Christian paradox, that he who loses his life shall find it. As one young lady put it, "Why didn't anybody tell me it could be like this?" When every thought, every emotion, every possession, every desire, is yielded to God, then the abundant life begins. And it has a richness and a fullness to it that many have learned to know well and which justifies our promise to you, "There's more."

# CHAPTER TWO

## *MORE LOVE*

One of the gay lilting songs of the sixties said, "What the world needs now is love, sweet love," and this judgment of the world which our young people have been so ready to make is not only correct, it is obviously correct. To look at the world today is to know that it needs love.

Indeed, if I look at myself, I know right away that I need love. I cannot live unless I believe that someone cares whether I live or not. I cannot grow unless I believe that my growth is important to someone. I cannot stand my pain unless I know that another shares my hurt in some measure.

Experts have learned that unwanted babies in foundling homes sicken and are fretful despite expert care. Even an infant who cannot yet reason needs love and responds to love and reacts unfavorably when love is not present.

Love, love, love—it's love that makes the world go 'round, it's love that keeps this whole mess from coming unstuck and disintegrating into chaos. And beloved, the wonderful thing I have to tell you about love is . . . there's more.

A young couple came to me just after their first wedding anniversary. Their faces were shining as if they were still in the middle of their honeymoon. "Father Bob," they said, "we have learned so much about love in this past year, we wonder how we ever had the nerve to get married, loving each other no more than we did a year ago." And yet, they had been very much in love when they had come to me for their marriage instructions and for the wedding. Until you have begun to experience some of the heights and depths of which this grand passion is capable, you cannot know the richness of the blessings that are in store for you.

Of all the things of which "there's more," in the abundant

life Christ promised us, love is the first thing that hits us. Putting aside all formal religious ceremonies for the moment, whenever a person really and truly takes Jesus Christ into his heart, wholly and completely surrenders his life to the Lordship of the Savior, the one unfailing sign by which we can know this surrender from without is the marked increase of love in his life.

He may manifest an increase in any number of spiritual gifts or fruits, many of which we will describe in subsequent chapters. But always and invariably, there is love. Jesus said, "If you cannot love your brother whom you have seen, how can you love God whom you have not seen?"

God is love, and those whose lives become possessed by the Spirit of God exhibit love. If they do not, they have not the Spirit of God. It's as simple as that. Show me a long-faced, self-centered, withdrawn Christian, and I'll show you a person who has only gone through the motions of surrender. Show me a person who is concerned with the minutiae of sacrament and ceremony and has not love, and I'll show you tinkling brass and a clanging cymbal. Years ago, I heard about a minister who was proud of having introduced some new ceremonies into his church, with a resultant loss of less than ten percent of his membership. Could this have been done from the love of God? On the other side of the pulpit was the lady I once met who said she never came to the Lord's Supper because she wanted to come fasting, and the service was too late in the day for her to abstain from food. Both had surrendered, not to God, but to ritual observances.

Love is a dead giveaway for the Christian. How many times have I heard a newborn Christian described and someone has said, "All of a sudden, she just lit up like a Christmas tree." Sometimes born-again Christians are described as "the shining ones." What is it that shines? It is the love of God shining out of their entire personality. They are transformed, not conformed; they are changed by what has happened inside, not by something external.

Now we all know something about love, just as we know something about breathing and eating—things we must know to stay alive. But you can breathe without breathing correctly or without knowing the refinements of the breathing exercises of yoga. And you can eat without eating correctly, certainly without the subtle delights known only to the true gourmet. And thus we all need love, and we try in our crippled way to give love, but dearly beloved, there's more.

We are told as Christians that we must love people whom we can't even like. That's all very well to say as a principle, but have you ever tried to do it? You find out very quickly that you can't love "by the numbers," so to speak. You can't turn love on just because you want to. Love is one of the gifts of God: if you haven't received His gift, you can't love; if you have, you can.

We are told that there are natural situations in which it is normal for us to love. We expect love within the family— between father and mother and brother and sister and parent and offspring. And what do we get? Some of the most heart-rending situations with which a pastor has to deal occur because love is lacking in the supposedly civilized family. Each week dozens of people come to me for prayer to mend broken relationships with those with whom love ought to be a natural and normal thing.

How many times have we seen a puzzled parent, confused by the seeming ingratitude of the son to whom he has given every "thing," to whom he has laid down the law in no uncertain terms. Many things that Christians do puzzle me, but nothing more than their attempt to solve interpersonal problems with intellect alone. You can no more think your way into a loving relationship than you can think your way into heaven. These things are of the heart; they are not contrary to reasonable procedures, but they are heart to heart, not just mind to mind. No amount of oratory can make up for a cold heart; no poem yet written is as eloquent as a gentle touch or an understanding smile.

Our minds are tools that we have been given to use. Our bodies are tools that we have been given to use. Our material possessions are things that we have been given to use. But the real me, the person that hides somewhere back behind these eyeballs, eventually gets through playing with all his toys, gets tired of manipulating all the material things he controls, and wants communion with other souls. And this is a communion that goes beyond a shared manipulation of physical things, beyond a meeting of the minds. This is a communion that knows love or the lack of it.

Some of our young people have been experimenting in recent years with so-called mind-stretching drugs. Leaving aside the hallucinations, the seeing of things that are not really there, we know that some drugs are taken in order to heighten the user's awareness of things, to sharpen the senses, to deepen the experience.

When I tell you that there's more to love than you know, I want to tell you that there's more in just this way. When you let the Spirit of God fill your life, you do find that the grass is greener, the sky bluer, and love sweeter than ever before. I wish you could hear, as I do, the testimonies of those who have this experience. The first time you kiss your husband or your wife after receiving the Holy Spirit, you have a new experience. A young woman in a church I served was filled one night with the Holy Spirit. Her husband happened to be away on a business trip. When she met his plane on his return and they kissed, he said, "Wow! What's happened to you?" You find that greeting a friend is different, and you see from his reaction that he senses something new in your feelings toward him.

There are some people who espouse Christianity who feel it their Christian duty to go out and help the unfortunate. And God certainly knows that the unfortunate need help. But precisely because He does know this, when you let Him take over your life, you find yourself led to help others, not because it is expected of you, not because it is the rule, but because your ever-loving heart simply bleeds for them. God is in you now, and the heart of God bleeds for the needy. If your heart beats with the heart of God, then you will long to help wherever you can.

Only those who have the love of God in their hearts can love the unlovable. When we see a picture of a Christian saint holding a leper in his arms, we say, "Oh, I could never do that." But do you know that the saint is unaware that he is doing anything unusual? My friends, we are all called to be saints, and the path to sainthood is simply to let the sanctifying love of God flood our hearts.

Need I point out that child, parent, or spouse — those who have a natural claim on our love — can themselves be completely unlovable at times? And it is at these times that they most need our love. We don't have it to give — but God does. If our blessed Jesus is living in and through us, then we can love; if He isn't, then we cannot. How simple it is.

Love is first and foremost. A gift given without love is an insult, a declaration of superiority.

Christmas is supposed to be the celebration of God's love in giving His Son; yet how much of our exchanging of gifts, how much of our giving, is not giving at all. How many people must you "remember" at Christmas for whom your gift is not a gift at all, but an expression of expediency or custom or of business necessity?

A reconciliation without love is no more than an armed truce, as precarious as a sword hung above your head by a thread. You can have everything else in the world, but if you have not love, you have nothing. Preoccupation with the things of the world traditionally crowds out love. And those who have spent much time surrounding themselves with things, traditionally are unhappy. Have you not seen them? Have you not read them? Heed and learn.

Love is not a thing; love is not an end in itself. Love is an action, a relationship, a movement between souls. You cannot love a "thing," because it is incapable of response. You can love only other souls — and God. God is the source and the end of our love. Love comes from Him and returns to Him. If the love of God is in us, all our other loves will be enriched and ennobled in a way we cannot imagine until it has happened to us.

Very well, then, I tell you that there's more, more love. It is fair to ask where it is, how can it be obtained. There is only one way. You must go to the source. There is only one source of love and that is our Heavenly Father. He so loved the world that He sent His Son. Jesus is love come to earth, love personified. He loved us enough to die for us.

The Spirit of love, the Spirit that comes from the Father and the Son, enters our lives whenever we are ready. We need merely offer the Lord Jesus the best belief of which we are capable — it need not be very much, just our best. Remember the man in the Bible who said, "Lord, I believe; help Thou my unbelief." Jesus will meet you where you are. We turn to Him and ask Him to come in and take over our life. And when we do this, He gives His Spirit. This Spirit, Who is above all the Spirit of love, comes into our very being and dwells there. And we become somebody else. We are never the same again. We can call it being born again, being converted, transformed, whatever we will, but we are new creatures in Him. He dwells in us and we in Him.

When this happens, beloved, you'll find out that there truly is more — more love.

# CHAPTER THREE

## *MORE JOY*

Not long after I received the baptism of the Holy Spirit, I had occasion to call a certain Baptist church. The young lady who answered the telephone was completely unknown to me, and we exchanged only three sentences as I asked for information about some matter. But after these three sentences, I dared to say to her, "Have you received the baptism of the Holy Spirit?" And she said, "Yes, I have. How did you know?"

One of the things that we ought to be able to see in a Spirit-filled Christian is more joy, more joy than he would otherwise have. It was the note of joy in the voice of this unknown secretary that convinced me that she had been filled with the Spirit of Christ.

Church members as such are usually not distinguishable from the rest of the population. It is not membership in an organization that fills one's heart with joy, even if that organization is the church. What fills your heart with joy is the presence of God's Spirit within you. And He is the Spirit of joy and of love and of power and of many other wonderful things.

I often think of St. Paul when he met the Ephesian Christians and said, "Have you received the Holy Spirit since you believed?" They had the correct password; they were professing members of the Christian faith. But Paul saw almost immediately that those things which mark the Spirit-filled Christian were missing in them.

Whenever I meet a bunch of gloomy, long-faced Christians, I want to say to them, "Have you received the Holy Spirit since you believed?" Whenever I hear church members carrying on like prophets of doom, I want to inquire if they have received all that was promised them when they gave their lives to Christ.

If you scan the New Testament, you will see the word "joy" repeated over and over again. I have recently visited many art galleries and have seen some of the most famous paintings in the world. I wonder how much these paintings have affected our thinking about our faith. For hundreds of years, the favorite subject of artists was religion. Yet you can look at dozens of paintings of religious people without finding one who is even smiling. Jesus said, "that your joy might be full." These artists seem to have painted only people whose cup of sorrow was full. How often do you see a picture of a smiling Jesus? I think such pictures are painted only by artists who know Him well.

Joy is a quiet thing; it is not ribald or raucous. Joy comes from within, and it is a spiritual quality. Joy is not an emotion that comes from glandular causes, nor from the satisfaction of bodily appetites. Joy proceeds from that on which your whole life is based. Joy is a reflection of the real you, and if your spirit is in harmony with the Spirit of God, then joy will proceed forth from your innermost being and will appear on the surface in various ways where people can see it.

There are professionally happy people who go about slapping everybody on the back and livening up whatever scene they come upon. If you happen to be feeling bad one day, it's very easy to resent this kind of person. These are people who put on an outward show of being a good fellow, of optimism, of laughter, even when they're dying inside. Theirs is not joy, but a surface counterfeit of it.

Christian joy is present even in the midst of difficulty. It would not be so unfeeling as to manifest itself in laughter in the presence of someone else's grief. It would not call on others to cheer up when there was really nothing cheery in their lives. But that Christian joy which dwells in our innermost beings remains there even when we are severely buffeted by the world in our outward lives.

There is a dry-cleaning establishment not far from where I live, and the woman who greets the public and handles the clothing is a small person who is crippled in her body. But she is not crippled in her mind, which is sharp, or her spirit, which is quietly joyful. Every day of her life, she has occasion to look at her body and be morose. Every time I've seen her, she has had a small quick smile. Thanks be to God.

Christian joy is irrepressible, because it comes from our loving Heavenly Father. No matter what knocks us down here on earth, in a day or two that power from within comes swirling back to the surface, wiping away our tears with the assurance that if God be for us, no one can stand against us.

The only things that threaten Christian joy are those same things that threaten our relationship with God Himself. God does not enter our lives uninvited, nor does He remain if He is not wanted. He will not remain in the presence of those things in our lives that are incompatible with His purity and love.

Thus I say to you that if you have once entered into the joy of the Lord, and now find it missing from your life, do not look for the explanation in the troubles that assail you from without. Look rather within, to that secret and most private place in your soul where the Spirit of God comes to dwell and irradiate your whole being. Is He there? Or is something else there whose presence has said to Him, "I no longer want you here, I have given place rather to another"?

It is not those things which come upon us daily from without that can kill the soul, but that which dwells within. God's joy does not come to us because all of our prayers have been answered to our exact satisfaction, but because we have paused in the midst of the world's hurly-burly and have invited Jesus Christ to come and dwell in our hearts. Where He is, there is the Spirit of love and of joy and of power. And where He is not, there the weight of the world will sooner or later reduce us to fear and sorrow and dullness.

Joy is an integral part of the abundant life that Jesus promised us. He who has the Son of God has life, and he who has not the Son of God has not life. This speaks of more than eternal life; it speaks of the life that we live now. Are you living or just existing? There is a popular expression these days in which those who find things suddenly going their way say, "Now we're living!" But that is still a life entirely under the effect of externals. Jesus comes to dwell within, and His light shines out through everything we do and everything we experience.

Look about you at those whom you know best. It is easy to separate the happy from the sad. But can you separate the happy from the joyful? Can you see the difference between those who are simply responding to the way the world treats them and those who have a glow coming from within? And where do you stand in this? Are you living your entire life just responding to that which comes upon you from without? Or do you have that welling up within you that affects everything that happens?

High on the list of the fruits of the Spirit is joy. It is a mark of one who has turned the control of His life over to the Son of God, of one who has become indwelt by the very Spirit of God Himself. It is one of the free gifts of God, and it can be yours today.

# CHAPTER FOUR

## *MORE PEACE*

"The peace of God which passeth all understanding . . ."
How often we wish for peace, how often we cry out for
peace, how often we seek peace as an escape from pressures
that have become almost unbearable. What does our faith
have to say to us about peace?

In Ecclesiastes (3:8) we find the phrase, "a time of war,
and a time of peace." So often we think of peace as being the
cessation of all activity. We long to withdraw from everything
that troubles us. We say, "Oh, if I could only get a little P
and Q," meaning peace and quiet.

Our church counsels us to come apart from the world from
time to time before we "come apart" completely. A retreat, a
quiet day, a withdrawal for contemplation and rest, is very
much worthwhile. Jesus took His disciples apart from the
world so that they could rest and meditate, seeking understanding of all they had seen and heard. Some of the reasons
for the anonymity of the city apartment dweller may be
found in the desire for peace. In an apartment with the
windows closed and the quiet hum of the airconditioner
masking all outside sounds, there is a kind of peace that is
based on withdrawal, on escape.

The more hectic the pace of our society grows, the more
this sort of peace will be desired. The noise level in our cities
is very high; the clamor for our attention by the various
forms of advertising hits us wherever we go. There is always
someone trying to sell us something or someone wanting us
to get out of their way so that they can do what they want-to
do. There is always the pressure to achieve, to measure up on

our jobs or even in the volunteer groups to which we belong. And a withdrawal from pressure can be called peace.

There is a story about a man who engaged native bearers and went on safari in Africa. And each day he pushed along at a record-breaking pace, driving the natives to travel farther and faster than ever before. One morning as he prepared to get underway, he found that the bearers were not making any move to go at all. He demanded an explanation from the head man, and was told, "Bwana, we have brought our bodies to this place too fast. We must wait here one day for our souls to catch up to us." How often we all need this, to stop and let our souls catch up to us!

There is another kind of peace which God allows us which does not involve withdrawal. I think this is the kind of peace of which the angel spoke at the birth of Christ, when he proclaimed, "peace on earth, good will toward men." I think this is the kind of peace mentioned in Philippians 4:11 when Paul says, "I have learned in whatsoever state I am, there to be content." Paul's life was certainly not one of withdrawal. He was whipped, taken into court, reviled, shipwrecked, widely traveled, prodigiously at work, and yet he was content. There is a kind of active peace called contentment.

In the old catechism of the Anglican Church, folks were called upon to do their duty in that state of life to which it had pleased God to call them. The enemies of this kind of peace are envy, jealousy, and covetousness. And all three of these, you may remember, are listed as deadly or soul-destroying sins. To want that which you do not have, to want it at the expense of others — this will kill the soul; and it will certainly kill any sense of peace you may have.

Contentment comes when you look at your active life and find it good, when you realize that what you are doing is worthwhile; if you are an achiever, that you are achieving at a satisfying rate; if you are a gatherer into barns, that you are gathering a goodly portion. The classic picture of the man sitting in a rocking chair at the end of the day with pipe and slippers shows a happy smile on the man's face. The smile comes not from the fact that he is resting, but from his knowledge that the day's activities were good.

The contentment kind of peace is a counting-your-blessings kind of peace; it is a grateful, thankful-to-God sort of peace. It is in connection with this peace that happiness comes. Happiness, the great American goal, can never be found by those who seek it, even though we are guaranteed the freedom to pursue happiness by our constitution. Happiness is always a by-product; happiness comes as the realization that you are where you ought to be, that you have what you ought to have, and that you are doing what you ought to be doing. You may amount to much or little; you may have much or little; you may be working very hard or very little; but contentment reflects your judgment that things are going as they should. And herein lies that elusive thing called happiness.

There is a third kind of peace which I believe is of supreme importance to the twentieth-century Christian. And this is peace viewed as harmony. Jesus said, "Blessed are the peacemakers," and I don't believe He meant those who make wars to cease. I believe He speaks here of those who help others to live and work together in harmony. I suppose the reason I believe this is because we clergymen spend so much time acting as peacemakers, and always in life's busy streets. To withdraw from discord is not peace, but an armistice, a truce. Neither of these is the same as peace.

To work together with one another, to play together, to build together, even to argue together to work out answers that must be found by dialogue — these things can be done in harmony and in peace. It seems to me that in this chaotic world in which we live, this is the most important kind of peace of all.

I somehow have a picture in my mind of Jesus going about His work with a quiet smile on His lips, a smile that indicated He was at peace. Yet He was on the go all the time, speaking to great throngs of people, healing the sick, struggling with demons, doing all sorts of very active things. In the midst of this, He had peace. Why? Because He was in harmony with Himself, with His mission, and with His God.

I don't care how busy you keep yourself, you will never be at peace with yourself as long as you are doing something that you know is wrong. You must seek God's guidance for your course of action and then follow that guidance or you will never have peace.

I don't care how skilled you become at manipulating people, getting them to do what you want, you will never find peace until you are in harmony with them, until you find some common motivating factor that allows you to work together with an honest sharing of goals. I know a businessman who is important enough in his company that he can shut himself in his office at 10:00 A.M. and at 3:00 P.M. and instruct his secretary to hold all calls. He does this in order to lift up to God for a few minutes all the responsibilities which are before him. Then his door is opened again, and he handles a frightening work load with ease and dispatch.

In music, harmony refers to the balanced action of two or more melodies. The emphasis is on the word action. We live in a world today in which the emphasis is on the word action. Never think that a Christian lives apart from the world; we live in the world, and God's power is available for us right where we live.

The third fruit of being filled with the Spirit of God is His peace that passeth understanding. It comes from being right with Him, being right with our jobs, and being right with the people with whom we live and work. With this Spirit and this peace, no matter how hard or how fast we go, we go with Him, and in Him there is peace.

# CHAPTER FIVE

## *MORE PATIENCE*

One of the fruits of the Spirit listed in Galatians 5 is long-suffering. Most of the newer translations use the word "patience" instead. As we use these words today, the distinction is important. Long-suffering seems to mean a mute enduring of continuing pain, while patience means the ability to remain in command of yourself while the solution for a situation is being found.

Once my son Ross and I were fishing, barefooted, and in old clothes, in a boat tied under a bridge in Florida's Indian River. While we were there, a very large boat went through the center span of the bridge without slowing down. Perhaps he didn't see us. In any event, his wake was tremendous and sent our boat crashing against the pilings. The first step I took to get my balance put my bare foot squarely on a fishing plug with three sharp treble hooks. I was in agony. But the safety of the boat had to come first. Somehow God gave me strength to handle the pain of the hooks in my foot and to do what was necessary to keep the boat from being smashed to bits against the concrete. When things quieted down, I was very glad to give my foot and its problem my full attention.

No one pretends that the life of a child of God is a life without pain. We have not been promised this at all. What we have been promised through Christ is a victory. And there is no victory where there is no struggle. Our faith does not deal with ways to escape reality, but with ways to bring our Christian armament to bear on the problems confronting us.

Part of that armament is patience. Most of us are too

impatient even to stop and analyze the meaning of the word. But I want to make such an analysis right now because I think it will open up some doors for us; I think it will point in a useful fashion toward some solutions.

We are all familiar with the problem of getting our balance in times of crisis. We get so shaken up by events that we can no longer think clearly, no longer make accurate evaluations of possible courses of conduct. In the simplest possible terms, we are unable to function effectively as human beings. Someone comes to my study for help. The problem is not insoluble, just too pressing for that person to be able to calm down and see the solution. Often, my task is simply to offer sympathy and prayer until the problem can be faced. Then the one who has to work out the solution is able to see what that solution is, and with God's help, to get to work on it.

A crisis has to do with a lot of pressure applied to us in a relatively short space of time. But we are also familiar with the experience of having a steady pressure applied to us over a long period of time. This has the effect of dulling our sensibilities so that we do not function effectively as rational beings in this kind of situation either. We either give up and feel that there is no solution to our problem, or we become so numb from repeated blows that we cease to seek for a solution and become what, in modern terminology, we might call "long-suffering." I don't think this state of being is what Paul had in mind at all.

God created us to be healthy, happy, human beings. Anything that takes away from our health, our happiness, or our humanity, is not of God. And when we become less than what we were created to be, God wants us restored and made whole. To this end, He has provided resources both within us and outside of us for us to use.

Our body has self-restoring and healing mechanisms built into it. Often the task of a physician is to free the body from outside interference so that these healing forces can get to work. Our minds bounce back after each period when we are "down in the dumps." We're made this way. We resist being reduced to the animal state; our humanity asserts itself in the climb upward and onward whenever something degrades us. We have these things inside us.

Many people count on their own built-in resources in time of trouble, either not believing that God has other powers for them, or, as in the case of so many Christians, not wanting to bother God with trifles. All we can say to this is that if something is important to you, it is important to God. Someone has pointed out that anything that bothers our children is important to us. Surely our Heavenly Father is no less interested in us. To save God for the big things only is to put a limit on His love. (Spirit-filled Christians may pray about a cut finger or the need for a parking space.)

When we are filled with God's Spirit, then His power also enters our lives. He will then work either through our own facilities, or He will lead us to others of His children who are willing to be used to help us. Thus, those who have the Spirit of Christ need not face their difficulties alone; they have the power of God within them and working for them in the lives of others.

Part of the meaning of patience lies in the ability to place our difficulties in the hands of others. A doctor treats patients who have submitted their difficulty to his care. Only a few people fail to recognize that God uses these men of science to do His work whether the doctor acknowledges Him or not. The point here is that the Christian is not torn by the dilemma suggested by Shakespeare when he had Hamlet say, "To be or not to be, that is the question. Whether it is nobler in the mind to suffer the slings and arrows of outrageous fortune or to take arms against a sea of troubles and by opposing, end them." Those who know not God might feel that they ought to suffer the slings and arrows of outrageous fortune, but the Christian is very explicitly expected to take arms against his troubles, and God provides him with the weapons.

There are mistaken Christians who do not know their own religion very well and who suffer from a martyr complex.

These are people who put on a wan smile and say weakly that we all have a cross we have to bear. This does dishonor to the cross of Jesus, which He shouldered gladly because it was part of a job He had to do. He did not submit meekly with the attitude that we all have to do a certain amount of suffering. He would have been glad not to suffer at all, as would any other honest person. But He suffered willingly in the course of His mission, just as a policemen or a fireman is ready to be wounded or hurt in the performance of his duty, avoids it if he can, but puts his duty first.

Cross-bearing is something else again. It is not meant to be used as an excuse for not doing anything about situations. Jesus' command to "pick up your cross and follow me" is a call to action, not an excuse for putting up with the unpleasant. Policemen, doctors, and firemen answer this call in a much more Christian fashion than most Christians. All of us have seen people who "enjoy poor health." You go to call on them and you get an "organ recital" — heart, liver, lungs, etc. These people wouldn't turn loose of their illness if they had a chance.

Kipling's "If" may have misled some people. "If you can keep your head when all about you are losing theirs . . . then you are a man, my son." Well, there's a bit more to it than that. Not only does the time come for all of us when our personal emotional circuits are overloaded, but God wants us to function as effectively as possible even when we are not overloaded, just loaded. The man who says he does not need any help, might consider how much better he would be doing if he had help. No matter how good a job you're doing, with God's help you can do better.

Another facet of the patience of a Spirit-filled person is his knowledge that if God be for him, he cannot ultimately fail. I believe it was Teddy Roosevelt who said, "Fear God and do your own part." I know he said to carry a big stick. That's all right — use the best powers you have, but fear God; that is, hold Him in awe and reverence and know that you are in the hollow of His hand. With this reassurance, you can cast aside worry, live with your fear, and get to work to do whatever can be done to change things.

The Serenity Prayer is not a "long-suffering" prayer:

"O God, grant me the grace to change the things that need to be changed, to accept the things that cannot be changed, and the wisdom to know the difference."

One who prays this prayer will constantly be analyzing the situation to see if obstacles are really insurmountable, asking God's guidance in the analysis and God's strength for the fight.

Life can be very hard indeed. No one denies this. But the grace and power of God is there for us. He never gives us any extra, by the way. We get just what we need, no more, no less. We have to give it every bit that we've got, and then count on Him for the rest. And when the moment comes, He's there – His strength is there, His guidance, and the heartening knowledge of His love.

The spiritual gift of patience, let me say again, does not consist of a meek submissiveness to a malign fate. It consists rather of looking at the situation, of accepting each facet of it as being exactly as good or as bad as it really is, and then saying, "All right, Lord, these are the facts; what do you want me to do with them?"

Days can be long and the nights longer. But for the Christian who truly opens his life to the indwelling Spirit of God, there's more of a very precious gift – patience.

# CHAPTER SIX

## *MORE KINDNESS*

When he wrote to the Ephesians, Paul said, "Be ye kind one to another, tenderhearted, forgiving one another, even as God, for Christ's sake, has forgiven you." Kindness is one of the fruits of the Spirit. When we meet someone who is kind, we know this kindness is of God, no matter what the religious background of the person. When we meet a church member who is habitually unkind, we know that the love and grace of God has not yet filled that person's heart.

The word kind has several meanings, and some of them are interrelated. One meaning is that two of a kind are of the same class or group and are therefore alike, having much in common. Part of the kindness that we display to other people, we show them because they are fellow humans. We are all members of one body, despite our outward divisions. So it is this recognition of kinship that is responsible for part of the goodness we show others when we are being kind. Being filled with God's Spirit makes this kinship apparent to us. We are all His children.

The story of the Good Samaritan illustrates the way people look for this kind of kinship, and failing to see it, turn away. Those who saw the man who had been beaten and robbed and then passed by on the other side of the road, might have stopped had he been of their class or group. The Samaritan stopped because he saw a fellow human in trouble; he sensed kinship on a very broad level.

Kindness often takes the form of sympathy. Sympathy, truly understood, includes sharing another's joys as well as his sorrows. As we point out in other chapters, one of the results of being indwelt by the Spirit is the ability to get out of oneself, to be saved from the inward-turning selfishness that makes us blind to every need that is not tied up with our own. In the freedom of the Spirit, it is possible for us to turn to other people with true interest. We can forget about our own needs for a while because we have truly turned them over to Jesus. They are taken care of. More than this, sympathy means putting ourselves in the place of another. We are able to cross the gap that separates two souls in this life, because of the presence of Christ within us. As He knows what is in the heart of another, so we can know also. A Spanish expression for, "I am sorry," translates literally into English as, "I feel it." Thus the Spirit-filled Christian is saying, "I feel what you feel"; this is true and kind sympathy.

Kindness, too, is a matter of being able to react to other people and their actions in a way that ministers to their needs rather than your own. This outward focusing of attention results in quite a different response to the actions of others than is usual. Not only is forgiveness extended when they trespass, but the understanding of their real needs leads to a positive response, something designed to help rather than merely to react.

In one town where I lived, there was a tiny little store on the corner. Its supplies were limited, though of great variety. The appealing thing about this little shop was its proprietor. He asked us to call him Duke because he was "no 'count." Duke was interested in everybody. He never talked about himself, but when it came your turn to be waited on, you felt that you had Duke's full attention, that there was nothing more important in his life than your well-being. Young people returning from college always stopped in to see Duke, because they valued his interest and were given value by it. So also did many adults, paying higher prices for his merchandise than in a larger store, but finding Duke's interest and kindness refreshing in a day of self-preoccupation.

Kindness involves trust. There are some situations in which

a kind response is taken as a sign of weakness, and we are made to pay dearly and unfairly by the one to whom we would have been kind. But kindness also involves opening our hearts to others, exposing our inner and tender feelings. This makes us very vulnerable in case they turn and rend us. Such a thing is not unknown. Jesus speaks of it when He says, "Blessed are ye when ye are persecuted for righteousness' sake." In the power of God we are willing to take this kind of a chance. And experience tells us that more often than not, the kindness will be appreciated. People who know little about God can nevertheless instinctively distinguish between the professional do-gooder and the unselfishly kind person who humbly offers to help.

On the third floor of the educational building in our parish, there is an unused classroom that we have converted to a bedroom. Its first occupant was an orphan who called himself the "Church Mouse." He was a college student who worked a bit around the parish in return for the room. Today he is in Thailand with the armed forces and looks on our church as a second home. The second occupant of this room was an alcoholic we were trying to help. This experience was not so good. He departed one night, leaving a heritage of hidden bottles, empty beer cans, and broken promises. As I write this, the room is occupied by a man just out of the state prison. He has a master key to the premises. There is some risk, but we are trusting God and counting anything the man might damage as expendable.

Not only is a kind person responsive in a reactive sense, but he is outgoing in an initiatory sense, that is, he sees needs and responds to them even when they are unexpressed. Almost any person will respond sympathetically when publicly presented with a need; not to do so would not look good at all. When the need of another impinges on our little world, when his need drives him to an action which affects us, then we are going to respond in reaction, and hopefully it will be a kind one. But the truly kind person is so outwardly aware, that he sees unexpressed needs in others and responds to them on his own initiative. For example, if someone who is deeply troubled comes to you and describes his trouble, you almost have to give him some sympathy. If someone else who is troubled mistreats you because of his preoccupation with his trouble, you at least have the option of being kind and forgiving. But here is another person who says nothing, and yet, if you are truly kind, you can sense that he is deeply troubled, and you will respond helpfully.

This ability to sense what others are feeling is God-given. But even when we know of a need, if it has not been forcibly brought to our attention, it is so easy just to go our way, shaking our head in sympathy but doing nothing else. We have all had the experience of trying to share a trouble of our own with someone, and instead of sympathy have received a recital of their troubles. But have we not also been in the presence of others who could help when we have been bleeding to death inside, but have not been able to communicate our need? Truly kind people reach out and discover needs wherever they go, and then go out of their way to assist.

Jesus was such a person. As we read the Gospel accounts of His ministry, we see that time and time again He saw beneath the surface; "He perceived that they were troubled," and He did something about it, despite His own needs, His own fatigue. When He comes to dwell in our hearts, His kindness becomes ours. It is one of the gifts of His indwelling Spirit.

# CHAPTER SEVEN

## *MORE GOODNESS*

The spiritual fruit of goodness is hard to describe except in human terms. We know what a good man is, and we can see the power of God at work in a human life, producing and maintaining what we call a "good man." Jesus said, "Why call ye me good, there is no one good but the Father." But this is to say that the ultimate standard of goodness is in God, who created all things. Therefore, when we call a man good on this earth, we are saying that he has begun to mirror, however imperfectly, that perfect goodness which is God's.

This is one of the things that happens in a life so yielded to God that God's Spirit has come in and is beginning to guide, inspire, and empower that life. In direct proportion to its yielding to God, we see the goodness of God in it.

Let's be very careful to distinguish between the goodness that comes from being indwelt by God and the goodness of men who work very hard at being good. Some people are so good that you just want to kick them in the seat of the pants. Deliver us, O Lord, from the professionally "good" people. They work hard at acting like Christians, but turn out to be only actors, not Christians, and ham actors at that. Their pious protestations of self-denial and altruistic motives do not ring true. The worst trouble with them is that they tend to overawe those of us who know how far we yet have to go to be good.

I suppose the first thing we notice about a good person is that he is other-centered. This basic mark of the Spirit-filled person results in a concern for our well-being that is bound to make us favorably disposed toward the good person. He just never seems to think of himself; he's always thinking of the needs of others and trying to be helpful. You know people like this; their whole life is wrapped up in doing for the other fellow.

Two things make the Spirit-filled person other-centered. The first thing, of course, is that God seeks people who will let Him work through them for the aid and comfort of His other children. Thus, when we let Him have our lives to use, when Jesus becomes incarnate in our minds and bodies, then His work will be done in the world through us. This means an outreaching that is part of the gift of goodness. (Let's remember that this fruit of the Spirit is also a gift in that it comes from God and is distinguished from trying to be good in our own strength.)

The second thing that makes the Spirit-filled person other-centered is his built-in security blanket. He can afford to be other-centered because he is so secure himself. He has given Jesus all his hang-ups, all his problems. He has turned over the guidance of his entire life to Someone who can handle it far better than he. So he is able to think about others; he has no need to be concerned for himself; he has yielded that basic worry by dying to self in Jesus.

Thus it is that the fellow whom we call good is the fellow who is responding to our needs instead of his own. He is free to do this because his own needs are being well taken care of. And he wants to respond to the needs of others because he is being programmed by the Holy Spirit, because his guidance system turns him outward constantly, and he finds his joy and satisfaction in helping meet the needs of others. His joy and satisfaction are closely allied with those of his Master.

We like to be around "good" people. We just naturally expand and bloom under their friendly interest. We say in another place that no one counterfeits worthless gifts. This natural liking for good people is motive enough for those who seek our allegiance for selfish purposes to learn how to counterfeit an interest in our concerns. Anyone who would control others or use others or get something from them is likely to seek first to convince them that he has their best interests at heart. The good person really does.

Another reason we like to be around "good" people is that they are no burden to us. Our human nature resents any pressure upon itself to do for others, and no matter how far we have come in our own Christian walk, we probably still have enough of this in us that we enjoy relaxing with someone who doesn't want a blessed thing from us. This is where the spiritually good person and the professionally good one part company. The man whose real motivation is the feathering of his own nest, will sooner or later pressure us for something that he wants. His goodness is a come-on, bait for his trap, which he springs when the time is right. The one who has the spiritual gift of goodness has no axe of his own to grind, now or later.

Let this knowledge of good people teach you something of God. He is harder to know since God is Spirit, but you can relax with Him because He is good. He wants good things for you, but He has no ulterior motive in His conversations with you. You can come into His presence with calm and with peace because He really cares only for you; He wants nothing for Himself. His greatest pleasure is to see you become what He created you to be.

The old gods of mythology were human in this respect; they had their needs and were therefore capricious. You could not be sure how they would react to something done on earth, because they had their own thing going up where they were, and much depended on the mood in which you caught them. Not so with our God, we have learned. He is not a projection of our human natures, but the Author of them, an Author who sees us as we are, only on the way to becoming something more.

We use the word good to refer to that which has a beneficial effect on our lives. If we use the word carefully, we mean those things which are moving us in the direction we believe God wants us to go. A shortsighted person might divide into good and bad those results he encountered as they compare to the goals he had set up. But we speak here of God's gift of goodness, of the fruit of goodness that one finds when God takes over a life. Therefore, the designation must refer to God's plan.

And finally, the word good has to imply a standard which exists independently of any of us. Immanuel Kant pointed out that moral judgments are always universals, that is, if we believe a thing is right, we think it is right for everybody. In these days of situation ethics, it becomes rather difficult to know right from wrong. But if it is truly God's world, then there is a standard, and it is His standard, and that ought to be our goal. I believe that when we yield our lives to Him, this standard becomes our standard, not just as an outward set of rules to which we feel led to conform, but as a course of conduct that we are motivated to follow because the Spirit of God within us points in that way.

The fruit of goodness then leads us to do God's will, to follow the right, and to be concerned with the needs of others because our own needs have already been provided for.

# CHAPTER EIGHT

## *MORE FAITHFULNESS*

One of the fruits of the Spirit that is highly prized in every era is faithfulness. Faithfulness has two meanings for us, the quality of enduring trustworthiness and the quality of enduring stewardship. In other words, when we say a man is faithful, we mean that we not only know that he will be where he is supposed to be, but that he will be doing what he is supposed to be doing. He is the man who answers, "yes," to the cry of "Keep the faith, baby." He is faithful, and he does keep it. The figure of the faithful retainer is familiar to all of us. He is the one who is always there, whose character is such that his acts are predictable; he is a point of reference in a world that may otherwise be chaotic.

The gift of faith is one of the nine gifts of the Spirit listed in I Corinthians 12, and the quality of faithfulness is one of the fruits of the Spirit described by St. Paul in Galatians. Obviously, faithfulness means that one is full of faith, so faithfulness would be a natural fruit or result of the gift of faith. But there's a good bit more to it than that.

Paul says that it is required of stewards that a man be found faithful. By this he means that one to whom responsibility is entrusted must live up to the trust placed in him. Well, we are all stewards in one way or another. Perhaps in our business we have things entrusted to us — responsibilities, money, even the lives of others. In our friendships we entrust our secrets, our emotional health, to others, and we trust them to be faithful. In our homes, most breakdowns of relationships are due to unfaithfulness, not necessarily in the sexual realm, but in every aspect of living together with another person. We have to be able to count on people, and we ourselves are depended upon by others. Hence faithfulness is a quality to be prized.

Faithful, as meaning trustworthy, requires first that we be devoted to that with which we are entrusted, and secondly, that we endure and remain faithful through thick and thin. The only true way to know if a man is honest is to observe his actions over a long period of time. One cannot be sure that he will endure until after he has been truly tempted. It takes a real devotion to a person or to a cause to continue faithful when inducements are offered not to be. This can apply to your business, your marriage, your personal life.

Faithfulness is tied in very closely with the degree of our commitment. If we are to be faithful to our Christian profession, then we must be fully committed to Jesus Christ. This is why faithfulness is one of the fruits shown in the life of a committed Christian who receives the gift of God's Spirit when he makes his commitment.

Now commitment implies other-centeredness as distinguished from self-centeredness. If your attention is on yourself, then the gratification of self will be your highest aim. Faithfulness is then impossible, because you switch your allegiance moment by moment to that which gives the most immediate gratification. To be faithful is to remain true regardless of personal feelings. When we say of someone, "You can count on faithful old so-and-so," we mean that no matter what happens to him, he will let nothing stand in the way of doing what he has committed himself to do.

Once in a while, we hear of a dog whose commitment leads him to say no to all the primary needs for food and water. A dog makes a commitment to his master which exemplifies blind trust at his level. Cases come to light where the master has died or been lost, and the dog remains on the spot, neither eating nor drinking until his primary commitment can somehow be fulfilled. Christians who fast sometimes do this as an exercise in putting their primary commitment first.

In every realm of our lives, the basic commitment to Christ

strengthens and illumines all of our other commitments. If we cannot be faithful to Him, we will find it extremely difficult to be faithful to our spouse, our business, or our friend. If we are faithful to Him, strength is given us to resist temptation and overcome that evil which would cause us to be unfaithful.

In His wisdom, God has given us certain helps for remaining faithful. God knows we get bored with it all; we want a change, we want to chuck the whole thing – we are tempted over and over again. He is our loving Heavenly Father, and He is quite aware of our struggle to be what we're supposed to be, day in and day out. It's easy to show great faith on great occasions, but hour after hour for twenty days, twenty months, twenty years . . .? But the gift of faith is there for us.

Regular prayer is an absolute must if a man is to be found faithful. And when do you most need to pray? When you have a great problem? When great occasions face you? It is good to pray then, but you most need to pray when you least feel like praying. It is in these moments that our faithfulness slips away, these moments when we couldn't care less about our responsibilities, the times when we want to chuck it all and go fishing or go buy a new hat or whatever our particular escape is. This is the time to be in prayer, like it or not.

There is also a need for regular Christian fellowship on something deeper than the Sunday morning worship level. Through such fellowship, God speaks to us, guiding us in our perplexities and reinforcing in us those characteristics which keep us faithful. Forego this fellowship, and you will soon begin to vacillate, to slide away from your commitments. The faithful one, the man you can always count on, you can always count on to be among the fellowship. He's not only helping you by being there, but he is being fed in a deep and necessary way himself. Time and time again, I have seen Christians sit in a sharing circle and have heard a person on one side of the circle minister to the needs of someone on the other side. Often the one whom God is using in this way is quite unaware of the need being met through him. But he is faithful in being an open channel, and God faithfully uses such channels to sustain His children.

Faithfulness begins with the gift of faith, and in the gift of faith comes contentment. You have made a number of commitments in your life, some consciously and some unconsciously. Examine them in the sweet light of Christ's love, be certain that you are walking in the will of God, and then ask His help to be found faithful. You can count on that help, because when all else is in chaos, God is faithful still.

# CHAPTER NINE

## *MORE GENTLENESS*

In the first chapter of James we read the famous text, "Every good gift and every perfect gift is from above, and cometh down from the Father of lights, with whom is no variableness, neither shadow of turning."

The fruits of the Spirit are gifts of God. They come to us from His bounty and His mercy and are not ours by right but by privilege. One of these fruits is gentleness. Not much is said in our culture about gentleness, but since it is one of the fruits of the Spirit, it ought to be acknowledged as a gift of God and should have our careful consideration. I call to mind some of the great Christians I have known. Some of them are famous, some are not known outside their hometown. Some have tremendous drive, others are quiet people. But all have the quality of gentleness; a soul laid bare before them can be assured of a gentle touch.

I would ask you first to put aside certain preconceptions about gentleness. The ones most damaging to an understanding of this gift are those associated with the concept of gentleman and gentlewoman. Like most of our words, these terms have a literal meaning in their origins but have come to take on other meanings which are not the same thing at all. Thus, to say that someone is of gentle birth is to use the words in a social sense that is quite far removed from the original meaning. We see well-researched movies today in which highborn people are pictured with not only atrocious manners by our standards, but with a lack of consideration for others that cries out "roughshod" rather than "gentle."

I think that gentleness can be considered both positively

and negatively. In its negative aspect, gentleness is the desire to avoid inflicting harm. You can pick up a newborn baby gently so that you will not hurt it. You can handle a priceless art object in the same way.

The desire not to inflict harm can be a part of a very positive Christian motivation to do good. As we go through the necessary motions of our daily life and are inspired of God to do things, we must often do them gently to avoid harming the very ones we want to help. This applies to personal relationships as well as physical ones.

But as we go deeper into our analysis of gentleness, we see that it is other-centered, that our motivation in all our gentle actions is the welfare of another rather than of ourselves. The difference between the gentle Christian and the "gentle man" of society is that the Christian does what he does from inner compulsion, and the "gentle man" from outer conformity. There are times when the truly gentle thing to do flies in the face of the traditions of a "gentleman."

Perhaps it would be well to comment that most of our social customs have at their root the desire for quiet, peaceable, and harmonious relationships among men. But once established as a custom, these same acts can be used to wound and hurt, and are sometimes thus used in society today. Can you not think of a socially adept person who uses the customs of polite society as a means of wounding those he does not like? And equally, can't you think of a very plain person who deals with others in a gentle way, showing consideration even though he is lacking in social skills?

Another difference between the gentle Christian and the popularly styled "gentle man" is that the gentle Christian does what he does whether he can afford it or not, because he is really thinking about the other fellow.

When the concept of "gentle man" arose in society, it arose among those who had the wealth and power to practice more civilized acts, while the rest of the world was still scrambling for a living in an almost animal way.

The spiritual gift of gentleness is not dependent upon good

manners or social custom or leisure time or money or power. It is dependent upon a life filled with love, the kind of love that comes from God, whether acknowledged or not. One who loves is other-directed, other-centered. He acts for the welfare of others; he seeks not only to avoid harming them, but to help in positive ways whenever he can. And he does this without thought for himself, because that is not where his attention is.

The reason we see Jesus Christ as a gentle man is that He was genuinely concerned for others. He counted even His life unimportant in serving and helping others. Jesus was not gentle with sin, but He was gentle with sinners. He was not unselfconscious when it came to His mission, but He did not count personal cost when it was time to reach out to those in need.

Many people today who have rejected Christianity have done so because they view gentleness as a sign of weakness. This is a common mistake. But concern for others is not the same thing as a lack of purpose in life. The desire not to harm another does not rob one of ordinary intelligence.

Out of the spiritual gift of gentleness should flow good manners, socially acceptable conduct. But the motivation is all-important. Just as it is meaningless to be seen on your knees in a church pew every Sunday when you do not really mean to love and to serve God, so good manners by themselves do not make a gentle person, merely a socially skilled person who may be tremendously self-centered.

Gentleness is a direct cause of happiness. When Jesus said it was more blessed to give than to receive, He was describing the blessed state in which the giver finds himself. Gentleness is a motivation for giving. God is love. God gave His Son because He loved. The Spirit of His Son, entered into human beings today, makes them lovers of others, givers of themselves, gentle people in the true and best sense of the word.

# CHAPTER TEN

## *MORE SELF-CONTROL*

Have you ever had someone all figured out, had them "pegged," so to speak, only to find them doing something so completely out of character that it surprised you? When this happens, we often ask, "What's gotten into him?" or "What's come over him?" To be more accurate, we might have asked who was in control of his life in that moment.

The Galatian list of the fruits of the Spirit ends with the one called self-control. This may be contrasted with all the fleshly evils listed in the previous verse. For every evil, there is a corresponding virtue in the world. Evils are indulged in by a self out of control or under the wrong control.

We must be careful about the way we use these words. Sam Shoemaker used to say that conversion takes place when control of our lives passes from us to Jesus. The Bible tells us that those who receive Jesus as Lord receive the gift of the Spirit. Self-control, then, is not control of the self by itself, but by God.

I don't think there's any question but that our unruly selves need to be under control. We don't want to do the things we do, but we do them. We don't want to be involved in drunkenness, dissension, party spirit, enmity, and strife, but we are. What we need most is to be saved from these selves of ours. And it is precisely this salvation that Jesus offers when He endows us with His Holy Spirit.

The analogy of a horse and rider may help. A horse who forgets he is only a horse is in trouble. If he accepts his rider and follows his guidance, he can go far. The rider uses the reins to point the way, but leaves it to the horse to decide just where to plant his feet. Together, horse and rider can fulfill the horse's destiny. Given his head, the horse will do little but graze and chase the mares around the pasture. He may be quite content to do this even as some humans are quite content to run their own lives. But, beloved, there's more.

We are by nature self-centered. We may deliberately adopt altruistic policies, we may learn the ritually self-sacrificing courtesies of polite society, but at root our motivation for this is selfish. And because this is so, we find ourselves unable to wear perfectly the mask we have donned. The selfishness crops out, and we sin, against society and against our own best interests. Then we are haunted by guilt, guilt over our failure to measure up to our vision of what we might become. We may do pretty well at times, but until we accept the saddle and bridle, we will always betray our own best dream.

In American society today, there are many evidences that "the good I would, I do not, and that which I would not do, that I do." There are various substitutes for willpower to help us quit smoking, many gimmicks to help us trim the figures we ruin by overeating, many clubs and organizations in which membership will give us a strength and purpose we do not have by ourselves.

If we need any proof that we are naturally self-centered, we have only to examine our feelings about yielding control of our lives to another. We may agree to cooperate – this is called enlightened self-interest – but we do not wish to yield in all things. Our relationship with God goes much further in this than our relationship to a marriage partner. Marriage involves a yielding of self for the good of the marriage. But marriage is a fifty-fifty proposition between two equals. And the divorce rate indicates that even this level of personal sublimation is beyond the capabilities of a substantial portion of the population. One wonders how we can expect one hundred percent yielding to God.

Luckily for us, God is infinitely patient. He has all the time in the world. We can pull away from Him again and again, we can sin against our relationship with Him repeatedly, and He has in His love provided a way back. Unlike a marriage spouse, He harbors no resentment. He is even willing to help us handle our guilt feelings for having pulled away. He is expert at helping us to save face, something so indispensable to our human pride.

God is also patient with our weakness, with our spiritual clumsiness. It is one thing to seek to return to God in deep repentance, after willfully turning away. It is quite another thing for the well-intentioned to despair of ever getting through their prayers without "coldness of heart and wanderings of mind." Far more ex-Christians are simply lapsed, than are viciously at enmity with God. They just gave up and drifted away. God loves them no less.

St. Monica, mother of St. Augustine, prayed for her son daily through all the years when Augustine's reaction was, "Lord, make me holy, but not now." A profligate, wealthy, talented young man, Augustine was years in responding to the outstretched hand of God. When he did, one of the great men of the church began to grow to full stature.

Our thesis here is that the yielding of self is necessary because we can never control self unaided. There is an old prayer which speaks of God who puts into our hearts good desires. As we say in our chapter on cleansing, God easily puts aside things that have beset us for years. But more than this, when God plans our days for us, He leads us into the paths of righteousness; He fills our lives with such an abundance of good things that we lack nothing. If it is true that the devil finds work for idle hands, the life yielded to God will never have any space for this sort of idleness. In practice, the abundant life seems to include a full schedule.

Cameron Hawley, who writes books about American big business, portrays a coronary-prone executive in his book, *The Hurricane Years.* Pictured is a man whose drive has been ambition for his career and who, after achieving success, still drives himself without reason, often until he has a heart attack. How different is the motivation behind the abundant activities of a yielded Christian.

One who is filled with the Spirit of God has no room for a spirit of wickedness. Some of us formerly impatient people who have become relatively unflappable are such not in our own willpower but because we have launched ourselves on a new dimension, one in which we don't have to excite ourselves, because Someone Else is in overall charge. This may be the specific kind of self-control Paul spoke of.

There is also the refusal of God to let us rest. We are counseled never to grow weary of welldoing, but we do grow weary. We are impatient of results, we are despairing of success, we are too often rebuffed. But where our own willpower fails, where our own intellect says "forget it," where our own persistence comes to an end, God continues to lead and to guide. As He never gives up hope, so we find hope springing eternally in our own breasts. It is thus that things are achieved without pressure in God's own time, things which are beyond our vision, things which require more of us than our own discipline could provide.

Self-control and peace are not the same thing. The peace of God which goes beyond our intellect, and the patience which we can display when yielded to God's purpose, do not make us proof against God's needling when such is required to get us moving. Peace is not the same as rest, and while we may be quite at peace about our goals, God will not allow us to rest or to stray until we have achieved them. I think this is why so many of the nation's achievers, people who get things done, are becoming yielded Christians. They recognize that when their spirits are under the control of the Spirit of God, their abilities will be used to the utmost. How far this is from the mistaken view that our religion represents a withdrawal from reality. Quite the contrary, it demands an immersion in it.

Therefore, Christians are right in the thick of things, working and striving mightily, not in their own power but in His, and not under their own control but His. It is because of this that we say with St. Paul, "No longer I live, but Christ liveth in me."

# CHAPTER ELEVEN

## *THE GIFTS OF THE SPIRIT*

No matter how wonderful a human character we may develop with the help of God, we are still not equipped for the life we have to lead in this world. Just as God's will for our lives cannot be carried out without God's help, so God's will for the world cannot be carried out through us without that help. And for this, He gives His gifts of the Spirit.

There must be some point in time at which the developing Christian begins to see his life with God as one in which the Christian is servant rather than master. We find persons who spend much of their time in prayer, attending prayer groups and other religious activities, who yet go to God constantly for help in carrying out their own will, not His. An observer sees instantly in their prayers a desire to use God, to maneuver Him into doing what they want. And their desire for knowledge of prayer and spiritual gifts has for its ultimate end the gratification of their own plan for life. Needless to say, such prayers are unsuccessful. What a waste of time to belabor God with prayers for things that God never told us to ask for in the first place.

John Kennedy, in an inaugural address, used the now famous lines, "Ask not what your country can do for you, ask what you can do for your country." Doubtless we clergy have been guilty of selling people on religion by telling them what God can do for their lives. But somewhere along the line we all have to realize that we were not put on this earth solely for self-gratification. There is a job to do.

St. Paul seems to have begun his public ministry as a rabbi at what might be called the second stage in the development of a religious person. Saul, as he was then, sought to mold his life according to the precepts of the law. He had great zeal for the law and began persecuting Christians because he regarded them as detractors from it. But this kind of religious life, though strenuous, has no goal other than conformity. In thanksgiving for creation and blessings, one tries to conform his life to a preset pattern given in a traditional law. This does not produce a radiant, joyful Christian. A TV comic said recently that some Christians spend so much time molding themselves that they end up as moldy Christians.

Jesus calls on us to be transformed, to come to newness of life in Him. And in this life, instead of being conformed to some outward standard, we are so filled with His Spirit that we are transformed into something new, a person who no longer lives for himself but Christ liveth in him. It is not too much to say that there is a second coming of Christ for each individual on the day that that individual opens his heart to the Savior and becomes indwelt, taken over, possessed, by Christ's Spirit.

Now when this happens, the work that Christ wants done in the world is done through the only bodies that Christ has today in the world — yours and mine. Those who are filled with His Spirit make up the total body of Christ in the world today. We must not be misled by the fact that the organized church calls itself the Body of Christ. Ideally, it is. Practically, those members of the church who are not Spirit-filled are members of the body who have atrophied, who are nerveless, powerless, useless, and dead.

When Christ's limp body that was taken down from the cross was wrapped for burial, it was handled with great reverence and love. And so we feel toward the church today. But Christ's fleshly body was dead at that point in time and remained dead until the power of the Father breathed life into it again. No matter how we may be conformed to the requirements, the rites, and ceremonies of the organizational church, we are dead until we become transformed by the renewing of our lives in Christ Jesus. Going to church, giving to the church, working for the church, all these are empty things that any pagan could do as well as Christians, unless they are inspired by the indwelling presence of the Christ.

A young marine named Phil was terribly injured in a training accident. When he was brought to our church, he was carried on the back of a friend. His body was emaciated, his legs wouldn't function, and physically he was altogether a mess. They brought Phil into the church where I was to pray for people, and left him propped up against a railing. I know that you are supposed to pray believing, but looking at Phil, I found it difficult to believe that God could do anything. Doctors had said there was no hope. Then I was led to pray in this way: "Lord Jesus, we know what You would do if You were here. You would lay Your hands on Phil and heal him. You have promised that whenever we gather in Your name, You will be there in our midst." I put out my hands: "Lord Jesus, use my hands – for Phil." The next day Phil stood alone and unaided for the first time, and began to try to develop strength in his wasted muscles.

Once the Lord Jesus comes into our lives, then life is a very different thing indeed. When no longer we live, but He liveth in us, then He says to us, "I want that person prayed for in order that he may be healed," and we have to go pray. For this we need holy boldness, but we also need the gift of healing that Jesus had. And if He sends us on such a mission, He will see to it that we have the power gifts that we need to do His job.

The nine gifts of the Spirit that are described in the following chapters are such power gifts. They are sometimes called ministry gifts because they are given to us to use profitably for the fellowship, for our ministry to all the children of God. There are three gifts of inspiration – tongues, interpretation of tongues, and prophecy; three gifts of revelation – the word of wisdom, the word of knowledge, and discerning of spirits; and three gifts of power – faith, the working of miracles, and healing.

Not all of these gifts are given to all people, but everyone who receives the Lord Jesus is given the ability to manifest some of them. Some gifts are much more common than others, and their distribution seems to indicate something about their relative value, for the most precious gifts are most rarely given. None of the gifts are given for the personal satisfaction of the believer, but are to be used in his ministry. The gifts appear only when the believer does his part to manifest them.

The current emphasis in many quarters on the gifts is often at the expense of emphasis on the Giver of the gifts. Despite lip service being given to the centrality of Christ, far too often people are being called upon to seek the gifts in order to prove that they have received the Spirit of Christ. This has been particularly true of the gift of tongues, which can be manifested under inspiration other than that of the Holy Spirit. To speak in some kind of jabberwocky does not mean that one has received the Holy Spirit of God; it proves only that one can speak in some kind of jabberwocky. But for one to yield his life so completely to the Lord Jesus that in the power of the Spirit he prays in a tongue, is another matter entirely. A life yielded to the Lord Jesus will have many other fruits and evidences by which one may judge the consecration of the believer, if judgment is one's goal. We have seen many people who love to speak aloud in tongues at public meetings whose attitude is judgmental, unloving, intolerant, and pharisaical. Some of these same things can also be said of some public manifestations of the supposed gifts of prophecy, interpretation, and healing.

In my travels I occasionally run into what I call a "goose-bump Christian." This is a person who comes for prayer seeking an experience rather than the Lord. I have seen these folks rise from prayer, shudder ecstatically and exclaim, "Oh, that one was a goodie!" Here again, the emphasis is on the gift rather than the Giver of all good gifts.

That gifts are misused or counterfeited is no reason to reject them, however. No one counterfeits valueless currency. It is a grave thing to play fast and loose with the things of

God, and those who do so must answer for it. The important consideration regarding the gifts of God is that they are gifts, and that it is our Heavenly Father who offers them. If we are to serve Him, we need them, and we must seek to manifest them. Let Him judge those who misuse them or counterfeit them, and let us get on with the ministry to which He calls us.

One more comment on the charismatic movement might be in order. The Greek word "charisma" means gifts, even though some newswriters today are using it to refer to a public aura of success. And where there are gifts, where power is being displayed, there will be criticism on the part of those to whom the idea of gifts is new or threatening. Someone has said that the average church today is so cold that if a normal Christian came in, folks would think he had a fever. Certainly very few churchmen are accustomed to regular prayer for miracles, and even less to seeing miracles occur. These things are frightening, and if proclaimed as a part of the normal Christian life, stand in unspoken judgment on those who do not have them in their own lives. Would to God that all church members believed and practiced the things described in the New Testament. But they do not, and some pastors even go to great lengths to explain why these things are not for today in order to show why they are not happening in a particular church. When they do begin to happen, then the old applecart has been upset, and there is likely to be a good deal of scurrying about and fussing. Christian charity, love, and understanding have not been markedly prevalent in some congregations where the gifts of God have begun to be evidenced. Even when the ones who are the recipients of the gifts have done their very best to avoid even the appearance of self-righteousness, those who do not have those gifts impute self-righteousness to them. Even where the gifts have been ministered in love, they have not always been received in love by fellow churchmen. I have heard a bishop say that he didn't want the Holy Spirit in his churches, because it was too divisive. The Holy Spirit is not an "it," but God Himself, and it is not He who is divisive, but those who seek to misuse His gifts, or those who, in the presence of the gifts, resent the implication that their Christian life still lacks something. Time and much love is needed to overcome these handicaps.

In a church where the gifts are known and practiced and where there is no dissension because of it, one woman who had received the Holy Spirit was approached by a friend who was evidently loaded for bear. She said to the woman, rather belligerently, "I hear you can speak in tongues. I suppose you think I ought to speak in tongues, too." The woman smiled and replied, "Oh no, I don't think that at all. I suppose God thought I needed this gift. I wish I had *your* gift of love." Well, what are you going to say to that? What can you say?

So as we go on to consider the gifts of the Spirit, it is well to remember that their effect is much different from that of the fruits of the Spirit. The world in general will be quite pleased to see the change in our characters as we manifest the fruits of the Spirit, which show God's power at work in us. But when we begin to manifest the gifts of the Spirit with love, by letting God's power work in the world through us, the reaction of the world may be rather different. But we can't stop there, there's more.

# CHAPTER TWELVE

## *THE GIFT OF WISDOM*

All of us have heard someone cry out in times of great stress, "Oh God, what shall I do?" Sometimes these cries are profane and not really addressed to God, but the anguish is real, and the desire for some kind of guidance, very real.

Uncertainty, the inability to know what we ought to do, is at the root of most of life's stressful situations. When we say we have problems, we don't really mean that we have difficult tasks, but that we face situations where our pathway is not plain to us.

One of the things that a pastor does in his counseling is to make choices clear. I think this is also true of a psychiatrist. Anyone who acts as the uninvolved third person in a marital dispute is there, not to tell the couple what they ought to do, but to help them to see what their choices really are.

Mrs. Hall and I have redecorated many old rectories. And we have always regarded this as an exercise in problem solving. The work we didn't mind, but trying to figure out what possibilities existed for redoing old houses was a stressful task. Once we accepted the situation as it was and canvassed the resources at our disposal to do something about it, we could usually come up with a plan of action. I think most people enjoy getting up in the morning to do a job if they know exactly what they are to do and how they are to do it.

The people you see going around with a harried look on their faces are the people who did not get up that morning knowing exactly what they had to do and how they were to do it. These are the people who are worried and anxious because they are literally lost souls. I don't mean that their souls have been lost to the devil, but that their lives lack an overriding sense of direction.

All of us face choices every hour of every day. We have to make decisions in order to live. What to eat, what to wear, where to go, what tasks to do first — these things make up our daily round and really do not disturb us at all. But we have to have a general goal, an overall purpose for the day or the week or the year, or else we are in trouble, even with the little things. A friend of mine is fond of saying, "Don't sweat the details." What he means is that if you have an overriding purpose in life, you will be pushing along toward your goal and won't get bogged down in minutiae on the way.

Now I submit to you that no one can help you with this overall purpose better than the God who created you. The divine gift of wisdom is given to us to show us where to go. It is actually a glimpse into the mind of God, a chance to see our lives from His viewpoint and to know what our true purpose and mission is.

Suppose you are traveling by boat along a stream. The banks of the stream are thickly forested; you can see only ahead and behind along the water. You cannot know what is around the next bend, and you can remember only what is around the last one. But if you had a friend in a balloon above you, he could see all the twists and turns of the river at a glance; and if you were in communication with him, you would soon see the whole picture as he did. We do have a Friend on high who sees the big picture. This is a gift, this is a relevation that comes to us, not because of our worthiness, but because our Heavenly Father loves us. We cannot earn it; we cannot deserve it. But we can be ready for it.

Some of us treat these gifts of God like a handbook on how to swim. We get hold of the book. We keep it on the shelf at home, and we display it if anyone asks about our swimming ability. Then when we fall into the water, we begin shouting for our book on how to swim and hope we can read it while learning to tread water.

It is highly probable that God has guidance for you at this very moment. I know people who receive His help for even the most minute details of their lives. You don't have to worry about bothering God with details; He's big enough and patient enough and loving enough to want you to know His perfect will for every tiny thing in your life. Don't wait for a crisis; don't wait until you fall in the water before you learn to swim.

Now obviously, it is no small thing to be given a glimpse into the mind of God. It is something to receive reverently and for which to be profoundly thankful. You need not save your reverence and your thankfulness for a sacred hour on Sunday morning. You ought to have communion with God in every hour of every day and particularly when you come to a fork in the road.

God gives us a gift of knowledge sometimes; He reveals to us things that He sees will be helpful to us in the job we are doing. But the gift of wisdom has to do with the future, with the ways we are to go. This is the road-map gift, the blueprint present from our loving Father.

I often tell about the man who went crying to God for guidance and lifted up many a wordy prayer saying, "O God, please show me what I am to do." And then suddenly he said, "Oh, never mind, God. I've just figured it out for myself." It did not occur to this ungrateful man that he had just received the gift for which he had asked.

When we are vouchsafed a glimpse into the divine mind, when we see clearly from the perspective of our Heavenly Father the direction that our life is to take in the next hour or year, we see this, and we understand this, with the equipment God has already given us. If you are going to think a situation through, prayerfully ask God to guide you. Use the mind He has given you. Then if your conclusions are not contrary to what you already know of God, you can thank Him for His help.

This help is much more readily available than most people know. Certainly it is offered much more freely than it is accepted. When I was a boy, I took my little brother to a movie. It was a cowboy movie starring Buck Jones. At one point the hero turned his back on the villain, and the bad man reached into his shirt and pulled out a pistol. At this, my brother shouted to the image on the screen, "Look out Buck! He's got a gun!"

Right now, God sees things in your life that you cannot see. Of His love, He offers the gift of wisdom to guide you in the days ahead. Learn to be open to the indwelling of His illuminating Spirit that you may receive the gift of wisdom and see your road as your Heavenly Father wishes you to see it.

# CHAPTER THIRTEEN

## *THE GIFT OF KNOWLEDGE*

In Jesus' final talks with His disciples just before His ascension, they began to understand many things that they had not realized before. One thing they acknowledged was that Jesus at this point knew all things. And they said this because at last they were truly aware of Who He was.

Jesus had been saying to them things like, "I and my Father are one," and "Ye who have seen me have seen the Father," but the disciples had been a long time coming to the realization that God had actually descended to earth, that a human body could be in this kind of relationship with the divine.

In whatever way we choose to describe God, one characteristic of God that we all agree on is His omniscience. This means that He has all knowledge, that He knows all facts that exist or have existed in time. Those who are devoted to science will notice that the word "omniscience" is made up of omni (all), and science (knowledge).

In other words, anything that is, is in the mind of God. We use the human word, mind, to indicate that which stores up facts and which is able to relate them to one another with the faculty we term intelligence. Just what the mind of God is like, is beyond our comprehension, since the smaller cannot understand the greater. But our concept of God includes the belief that all things are known to Him.

I think we are greatly helped in our understanding of the gift of knowledge nowadays by the science of cybernetics. Cybernetics is the study of the collecting and handling of facts by mechanical means; its end product is the computer.

Perhaps the simplest computer is the common adding machine, which possesses memory and the ability to combine facts to reach a conclusion. All computers must be programmed, that is, they must have the facts put into them by man, and the methods of dealing with the facts also built in.

The computer can never know more than its creators, although it can be designed to handle a volume of facts at a speed which is beyond human capability to duplicate. But no matter how complex and knowledgeable a computer may become, it is a creation of man.

I'm sure that all of you have had some contact with computers, either the ones in a bank which can check your account and report back at the pressing of a few buttons, or the ones in an airline which have access to the passenger and flight information of the entire airline system. What you see is not the computer itself, not the place where the information is stored, but one particular console which is connected to the computer in some way. From this console, the memory banks give forth their information, and the fact-sorting and relating machinery can be made to work.

Now, of course, I don't mean to imply that Jesus is a machine, but I do want to say that He has access to the information stored in the mind of God. He and the Father are one. In His human form, pinpointed in time and space, He is in a sense as the console is to the master computer. He is the part of the computer visible to us and able to produce all the information and perform all the operations possible to the central organ.

There is a vast difference between a warm and loving flesh-and-blood person and an impersonal machine. But our thinking and understanding are so conditioned to machine terms that I thought this illustration might be helpful.

One of the gifts which comes to us when we take Jesus into our lives is that we get hooked into the master computer, too. We don't get a full hook-up like Jesus has; I dare say it would burn out all our circuits. But some of the information in the mind of God is made available to us. This is called the gift of knowledge.

The gift of knowledge gives us information that we have not developed for ourselves. This gift concerns facts that exist; it has to do with the present and with the past and with the future. We come to know things about people or situations that are not based on our personal observation. This is supernatural knowledge, not human knowledge. It is not intuition, because intuition involves reaching conclusions based on observed data. That is a natural or human ability. The gift of knowledge gives us facts we did not have before.

The disciples finally knew that Jesus had this gift totally. Anything that a human mind could contain of that stored in the mind of God, Jesus had before Him. As we read the New Testament, we see many cases of this same kind of information being given to the early Christians. Peter was told that a centurion would seek him out; Ananias received information about the blinded Paul; Paul saw a man of Macedonia calling to him. I have had these supernatural revelations, and so have many of you. As we need to know things in order to carry out the ministry that God has for us, He reveals information that we could not come by in any other way. If you have not had this experience, think about it. It makes sense, doesn't it?

Our Father Who is in heaven has a will and a plan for His world. That plan is dependent on the readiness of His servants to carry it out. As we His servants offer ourselves to be used by Him, He puts into our minds those things which our limited vision cannot see or our human knowledge know. The gift of wisdom lets us see the pattern in the facts before us. The gift of knowledge gives us new facts.

When such knowledge comes, remember that it is given to you for a purpose. When you are seeking to do God's will, do not hesitate to ask for what knowledge you need. You are vastly more important to God than any machine, and in His love, He will give you what you need.

# CHAPTER FOURTEEN

## MORE FAITH

There's more to faith than you know, or than I know either. People tend to say, "Oh, I have a lot of faith," or "I don't have very much faith," as if this were a personal characteristic, a facet of our personalities.

But faith is a reality; it is a spiritual thing, but it has existence. The amount of it that you have in your own life is subject to change; it can be developed, broadened, deepened, extended to areas in which you now have no faith at all. No matter where you are in your journey of faith, there's more.

Faith is thought of by many as something very insubstantial, but there is nothing more important in life. Faith is the glue that holds a lot of other things together. Faith is regarded by some as a thing you either have or you don't have. But the faithless can become believers, and those with a shaky faith can go on to firm ground. "I believe, Lord; help Thou my unbelief."

Faith is a gift. You can prepare yourself to receive it, but you cannot pursue it and achieve it. Like all spiritual gifts, faith comes from God and rests upon God. You may study and work and fret to get more faith, but faith comes when you are ready to receive it from God as a free gift. "I believe; Lord, help Thou my unbelief."

Paul says that faith is the substance of things hoped for, the evidence of things not seen — things that exist only in our imagination, things that have not yet happened before our eyes so that they can occupy a place in our memories. These things have reality if we have faith. How else except with the

eyes of faith can one see that which the physical eyes have not yet seen?

Sometimes faith in physical things rests upon experience and probabilities. We see this illustrated in our driving of automobiles. When we come over a hill at high speed, we have faith that the road will be clear ahead, or that we will be able to stop if there is an obstruction. Who can drive a superhighway at night without faith that the road is clear? We all overdrive our headlights. A cement block in the road would kill us before we could swerve; yet we drive on in faith that the road will be clear of such things.

Sometimes faith in spiritual things rests upon spiritual experience. If we receive love from someone each time we meet him, we begin to have faith that we will always receive love. If God answers our prayers with a "yes" time after time, we begin to expect to receive that for which we ask each time we pray.

But faith that is based on rewards is an untested faith. Maturity in this world teaches us that we can expect the unexpected, that no realm of experience gives us an apparent one hundred percent result. We do not always receive what we ask God for: the most loving person we know will sometimes meet us with a rebuff; progress makes our mental certainties uncertainties; and one day we do drive over a hill and collide with an obstacle before we can avoid it. What happens to faith then?

This is where faith comes into its own. I do not know why God heals some of the people for whom I pray and apparently does not heal others. I feel sure that I have no right to demand that He explain His conduct to me. Why then do I bother to continue to pray? Am I just playing the odds? Not at all. My faith is not that God will heal every time; that contradicts the evidence that is before me. My faith is in God's call to me to pray for people who need healing. I place my faith in this call, and I pray. What happens then is up to God. I trust Him; I don't understand what He is doing all the time, but I trust Him as any child

must trust His Father. Without this trust, I have no basis for my life. That is what I call faith.

Experience has a lot to do with developing faith, but a tested faith is based on trust. A tested faith is one which says, "I believe anyhow." No matter how little evidence there is in a situation, no matter how little justification there seems to be for faith, a tested faith continues to believe. When I learned to fly an airplane on instruments, I was taught that the first principle of blind flying was to trust your instruments rather than your sense of balance. Those of us who were accustomed to "flying by the seat of our pants," found it difficult to believe the needle, ball, and airspeed indications when our inner ear told us we were doing something else entirely. The answer was, "Believe anyhow."

The reason for this gives us an insight into the true nature of faith. Faith based on a regularly repeated experience is not really faith at all, but simply a learned lesson. After so many times, you know what to expect. True faith doesn't know exactly what to expect, but trusts that it will be the right thing, because it will be the will of a loving Heavenly Father.

If I lift up my children to God in faith, I may be extremely puzzled by the things I see taking place in their lives. But my faith is in God and in His ultimate goodness; so I continue to entrust them to His care, not jerking them back from Him because He has failed to follow *my* plans.

Ultimately then, faith is reposed in a person, not in a series of events. And that person is God. We can have faith in other human beings, but will always be aware that they are fallible mortal persons who may, even with good intentions, let us down. But God is faithful, we can place our full faith in Him. He will never let us down. We may not understand, but we can totally trust. Have you ever tried to argue with someone, who had this kind of faith? No matter what evidence you marshall, they still continue to put their trust in the One they know.

When all is said and done, there is not very much difference between faith and commitment. When we say to a

person, "Oh, I wish I had your faith," perhaps what we are really saying is, "Oh, I wish I had committed my life as completely to God as you have."

The gift of faith comes with greater commitment. In other words, when you are ready to turn it all over to God, you are ready to trust Him, to have faith in Him. This means that you have faith in the ultimate outcome of any situation. This means that you are so yielded to His purpose that you are willing to keep on going, even when things *look* bad.

Faith is indeed a gift, but it is a gift that you can receive only when you are ready. I promise you that God wants to deepen your faith right now. But He has given you free will, and thus can only give you more faith when you are willing to trust Him more.

The reason many people find a great faith in a catastrophic situation is that great adversity is needed in their particular case to bring them to the point of giving up, of giving in to God, of turning the whole situation over to Him. When you have done this, then you trust in Him implicitly; you know you can't make it on your own; so you put the whole mess in His lap. And you have to trust Him. Out of World War II came the expression, "There are no atheists in foxholes." Many a person has turned to God when circumstances made it apparent that his personal resources were no longer adequate.

Why wait for such a thing? Let your intellect guide you to an answer without waiting for circumstances to beat you into submission. Our God is a good God. He loves us. Many things prove this, including things in your own life if you will but examine them. If this is so, then we can trust ourselves to God. We entrust ourselves to others for only two reasons – because they have something to gain by being helpful or because they love us. God has nothing to gain unless it is the fulfillment of His own nature, but He does love us. Therefore He desires the best for us. Whatever the situation, we can trustfully put it in His hands. I do a lot of flying as a passenger in commercial jets. It is my invariable custom as power is applied for takeoff to close my eyes for a moment and say, "Father, into Thy hands, I commend my spirit." I hope I never get too blase' to do this.

There are many things on your journey of faith that you cannot do until you have faith enough. Once God has showed His love for you, as He did in sending His Son Jesus, then you can put your trust in Him. He will reward this trust with an increase of faith.

Some people are concerned as to whether this growth in faith should be gradual or sudden. Much depends on your personality and your need. I heard the other day that there are two ways to get to the top of an oak tree: one is to start climbing; the other is to sit on an acorn for rather a long time. Undoubtedly a great many people have taken a tremendous stride forward in faith all at once, because they have all at once decided to turn the control of their lives over to Him. If you are going to let loose gradually, you can expect only a gradual buildup in trust. I think there is something to be said for a definite decision to yield, a decision taken after careful and reasonable consideration, but a decision that causes you to turn your life much more completely over to Him. After all, we are not sulky children to demand that God cajole us bit by bit with gifts of sweetness in order that we will gradually let down our guard. We have the power of choice; it is good for us to exercise it.

And when we do, we find that there's more — more faith.

# CHAPTER FIFTEEN

## *MORE HEALING*

The gift of healing is one of the nine spiritual gifts. Along with prophecy and tongues, it appears as one of the gifts whose results are immediately visible in the life of the person who receives it. Nothing will stir a man's interest in God like an experience of His power at work in this present time. And healing is one of those experiences that has been responsible for many a modern-day conversion.

Let us distinguish at the outset between healing and the gift of healing. The word healing is normally used in the passive sense except in the case of a doctor of medicine. And there are many, many, excellent books on Christian healing which describe the process of people being healed by God's power, with and without the company of medical science. Most healing today is done in full conjunction with those who work in the healing arts. When Christian healing is mentioned, usually it means the process by which one is healed.

The gift of healing mentioned in I Corinthians 12 uses the word healing in an active sense. The one who receives this gift is not healed, he heals — he becomes a healer. He does not do this in his own power, except in rare cases; he does this by becoming a channel for God's healing power. He is the channel, not the recipient of what flows in it. Nor is he the channel by his own skill except he be by coincidence a medical doctor or some other practitioner of man's healing arts. I remember one day when Virginia Lively, a Florida laywoman with a great gift of healing, came to speak on the subject of healing at a Faith at Work Conference. That she had a horrible cold was plainly evident in her appearance and her speech. She told us ruefully that she had had quite an argument with the Lord. "You know, Lord," Virginia had said, "that I can't get up in front of all these people and talk about healing in this condition. I can't be sick – I'm the healer!" But of course, she wasn't the healer, as she herself well knew, and the sight of her teaching and later praying for people who needed healing helped all of us understand the healer's role as a channel for God's power. (If it does not confuse the issue, we would like to remark that those who give themselves to be channels for God's healing power often find themselves being marvelously healed in the process. But it is also true that the healer can himself be much in need of healing and still be able to function as a channel, embarrassing as this might appear to be.)

Therefore, those who receive the Holy Spirit in His fullness need not expect to be healed of all their ailments by virtue of their new spiritual state. On the other hand, in this new world in which they find themselves, there are many pathways to spiritual growth to be explored, and healing is one of them. Anyone can turn directly to God through Jesus Christ and ask for healing. It is quite possible that the healing will come. But it is a fact of experience that when our own healing is needed, we are usually not at our best. We find it hard to pray, hard to be open to receive what God has to give, hard to be expectant. And this is where another person who also believes can be so helpful. He is not under the same burdens you are; therefore he can join with you in this matter and act as a channel for your healing. His faith undergirds yours, his expectancy makes up for your lack, and through him, your healing comes.

To receive the gift of healing is to be such a person, one who is ready to help others, to supply the faith and the expectancy that they lack, to offer his own strength in any way that it can be used in order to become a channel of healing for the one in need. This is a high calling for the Christian. It is not always an easy thing to do. It can be costly in terms of spiritual and physical strength. But it offers immediate rewards in terms of the knowledge that God's work is being done, and that you have the privilege of being used in some small way to do it.

Healing is needed in body, mind, and spirit. Those who are especially interested in this subject should read one of the excellent books available. You will find that faithful people are being healed or made whole in all three of these basic realms of our human existence.

Bodily ills are straightforward, measurable by the five senses, and it is usually quite apparent when a physical healing takes place. I paid a call on a sick parishioner in the hospital one day, and my praying with her evidently made an impression on her roommate, for she too asked for prayer. I prayed somewhat perfunctiorily as I remember, for I knew neither the person nor the problem. But God used my prayer nevertheless. The woman was suffering from high blood pressure and had had a high reading an hour or so earlier. Shortly after I left, another reading was taken, and it was normal. This grateful person called me a few days later and reported that her blood pressure had remained normal, and she was soon discharged from the hospital. Physical evidence had very quickly validated the action of God.

Illness of the mind is much more subtle, and because it sparks all sorts of emotional symptoms, is much more difficult to deal with. Yet one who feels called to be a channel for healing can lift up mental and emotional illness with the same confidence that he does bodily illness. It is not necessary to understand the illness to commit it to God's healing, but it is necessary to be understanding with the person who has it. Sympathy and loving concern help one to be an open channel for the healing of another.

I can recall so many whose lives have been transformed by the healing love of Christ. One person in particular, whom I shall call Leta, was bound. She was such a tight bundle of nerves and complexes that she was not fun to be with, could not relate to groups or persons, and was completely unable to express herself regarding her faith. After healing prayer and some healing of her memories, she became a different person. She is open and loving with her many friends; prayer groups meet in her home; and she has a freedom in witnessing that makes it hard to remember her former state.

Spiritual healing also works in the realm of the Spirit.

Laurie is a person who is not very abundantly blessed with this world's goods. She lives in what is euphemistically called "a transitional neighborhood," a racially mixed set of apartment houses not far from an urban renewal area. Laurie has no special theological training. She reads her Bible a lot, but would never call herself a Bible scholar. But Laurie cares — she cares about human need, she cares about persons, and she spends a lot of time talking to God about them. Because of this, Laurie has been used repeatedly to help people who are spiritually ill. She "hears their confessions," as one woman listens to another's tale of woe. She assures them of God's eternal forgiveness with all the confidence that a priest could display, and she helps them understand the ways of God as she herself has known Him. Not a professional in any sense, Laurie is a professing Christian whom God continues to use for the spiritual healing of His children.

One final word about this matter. If you are to be a channel for God's healing, then it is not often that you will give the treatment yourself. By this I mean that spiritual healing is not medical healing; you will pray for those sick in body, but you will not dose them with medicine. You will pray for those ill in mind, but you will not attempt to be an amateur psychiatrist. You will pray for those in spiritual sickness, but you will not hear their confession nor give them absolution. There are professionally trained people who can do all these things. But they have neither the time nor the inclination, most of them, to also make themselves available as a channel for God's healing.

A young housewife came to our altar rail for prayer one night. She reported that her doctor had found a lump in her neck and did not wish to treat it immediately because the treatment involved radiation, and the girl was pregnant. She didn't want to wait out her pregnancy for this healing, so came expectantly for prayer. We did pray for her and asked God to heal whatever was causing the lump. The lump disappeared immediately, and she went on her way rejoicing. Her doctor had also attended our service that night for the first time. She went to him, and he made a visual examination which he later confirmed in his office. There had been a healing, and the doctor is now a frequent visitor to our services as well as a member of the religion and health committee of the county medical association. Already a good chruchman, he now is even more open to be a channel for God's presence as he uses his medical skill.

Quite often your prayer for healing will lead the ill person to the right source of treatment. Sometimes the treatment already being given will become effective; sometimes the patient will begin to accept that treatment — to take his medicine, so to speak. Almost always, spiritual healing has its effect in conjunction with secular healing, whether in body, mind, or (pardon the word secular) spirit. In some cases healing takes place immediately, and no further treatment is necessary. In other cases where treatment has been ineffective, it becomes superfluous because healing is taking place without it. But anyone experiencing this gift should be very slow to counsel the giving up of expert help; this is beyond his competency.

The most common physical method of praying for healing is to lay hands on the person to be healed. A light touch of both hands upon the head or, if seemly, upon the affected part, is the most ancient and universally used external sign of healing. (Clergy may use consecrated oil, but this is a sacramental thing and beyond the calling of most lay people.) The laying on of hands is accompanied by prayer, and this prayer is better if it is as specific as possible. There are persons who have a great healing ministry who pray a short set prayer over each person, not seeking to know the specific need nor praying particularly about it. God does know the need before you enunciate it, and in large healing services a vast amount of time is needed to ask each person his need and then to pray for exactly that need. But the latter is our method, and we have found it more effective than the other, perhaps because we can be better channels if we know what we are being channels for. In any event, we suggest that you know what you are praying for, that you be quite specific about the need, and that you be equally careful not to tell God how He is to go about meeting that need. Just place it in His hands and expect action.

It should go without saying that when a professional in one of the healing arts also receives the spiritual gift of healing, wonderful things occur. Professionals include doctors, nurses, technicians, psychiatrists and psychologists, and yes, clergymen. But anyone who is willing can manifest the gift of healing after he receives the power of the Holy Spirit. Like all the other gifts, it depends on your taking the initiative and beginning in faith. Once you have done so, you put the results entirely in God's hands; you don't keep score; you don't try to collect medals; you remain a completely humble tool in the hands of God. The results will surprise you.

# CHAPTER SIXTEEN

## *THE WORKING OF MIRACLES*

How we twentieth-century people scoff at the idea of miracles! We say that they do not exist; we say that anything called a miracle could be explained away if only a more careful study were made of the occurrence. And yet we retain the word miracle in our language, and the most skeptical of us can be brought by a happening in our own experience to the point where we will exclaim, "It's a miracle!"

What is a miracle? How do we define this word? There are some who speak of miracles as if they were something that happened that could not happen, as if somehow the laws which govern our existence were suspended for a time so that this surprising event could take place. But this sort of definition leads to skepticism, because whether we call the laws of this world God's laws or nature's laws, we know that they are not suspended to help our individual causes. If the greatest saint in the world falls from a high place, we expect the law of gravity to operate until he is dashed to the earth below.

I would define a miracle as something which happens for which there is no explanation apparent at the time. A miracle is an event which so far exceeds human knowledge and human expectations as to put its explanation in another realm. We can try to understand, but in the end we can only shake our heads and mutter, "It's a miracle."

Not long after I received the baptism of the Holy Spirit, I was driving my car one day, and it occurred to me that I ought to go to a certain drugstore and see a certain lady. As I turned to go that way, I realized that I had no valid reason to do this; I had never seen her at this place and had no evidence to suggest that she would be there now. Yet I went. And sure enough, as I pulled up in front of the drugstore, she did too. I expressed my puzzlement at all this, and she said, "When are you going to learn to trust God?" There were forces at work here which went beyond human knowledge.

Now God has told us through the Apostle Paul that those who are filled with His Spirit may receive the gift of working of miracles. This is rather an awesome thing to contemplate, and most of us are certain that we do not deserve it. Yet those of us who make a total yielding of our lives through Jesus Christ are in line to become miracle workers. It may have happened to some of you already. And I can tell you this: those who expect miracles and seek miracles are much more likely to be involved in them. For those who ask, receive, and those who seek, find.

Since a miracle goes beyond human comprehension, it would be somewhat presumptuous of us to do a study which might be called "the anatomy of a miracle." But there are some things which we can understand, so let's take a look at them.

Let's look first at the normal or usual happenings with which man has to deal. These fall into two categories – those which man simply experiences passively, and those which he initiates and promotes. Miracles do take place in the first category, that is, in those things that just happen to man with no volition on his part at all. We can't say very much about these things except that in general we place ourselves completely in God's hands and trust everything that is beyond our control to Him.

But the miracles that we are concerned with here are those in which man is active himself. We are dealing with the gift of working of miracles, a human experience in which a person acts as a channel for the power of God in such a way that something happens which is beyond our understanding or our normal expectation. I believe there are some things that we can know about that will make us more ready to be used by God to do His miraculous works.

It is important that we begin by understanding the way humanly directed events usually proceed. I think there are five elements involved. They are concept, plan, equipment, drive, and luck. A humanly directed event begins with the concept, the germ of an idea, the suggestion of the possibility of action. Sometimes only a genius will see this possibility; sometimes the bare idea immediately brings the problem nine-tenths of the way to solution.

Next comes the plan. This is the working out of the basic idea, the visualizing of the courses of action available and the selection of the proper ones; this is the whole event hypothesized before any visible action takes place.

Next comes the equipment needed for the action. This may be something involving tons of physical matter, or it may be personal characteristics and qualities, all depending upon the contemplated event.

Fourthly, there is what I have termed drive. The world is full of plans, many of them carefully worked out on paper, that never came off because the resolution and push needed to get the event started and prosecuted to its conclusion was not present. Many of us have the talent for great artistic achievement but do not have the drive necessary for the hours and days and months of practice that lead to the technical excellence necessary to artistic expression. Most people feel that they could write a book. But you have only to try to write a book to find that book is fairly easy to conceive and plan, that it is not too hard to find a typewriter and paper, or even to get the language skills with which to express your ideas. But to sit down to work day after day is another matter entirely.

And the last thing is what we humans call luck. No matter how carefully you plan, no matter how excellent your equipment or firm your resolve, yours is not the only project in the world. There are natural laws, civil laws, and the desires of others to consider. For our plan to work, we have to have what we sometimes call "the breaks." And here many plans have faltered because as they progressed, it seemed as if everything was against them, and they finally wore themselves out battling a hostile world.

Take a concept as a grandiose as putting a man on the moon for the first time. The very idea is staggering, yet once it is entertained, those who have the necessary skills can begin to plan. Then equipment for the flight and for the men must be assembled and tested. There will be many disappointments, many setbacks, but with sufficient resolution the plan will go forward. Finally comes the big day of the launch. Will the weather be good? Will one of the astronauts fall ill? Luck holds, the rocket is launched, and man takes a step forward in his exploration of space.

It is against this kind of background that I want us to consider the spiritual gift of working of miracles. What happens when a human being no longer lives but Christ liveth in Him? What happens when the power of God is working in a human life that is yielded to Him?

Think first of the concept, the germ of the idea. Those who take their problems and activities to God in prayer find themselves with hundreds of ideas that they never had before. We who cannot see around the next bend in the river are in contact through prayer with One Who can. And as we begin to expand on the basic idea and evolve our plan of action, we have His help and guidance, every step of the way.

Once the vestry of my parish faced a problem. We chewed at it and got nowhere. Finally, one of the men said, "I'm sure God has an answer for this somehow," so we prayed about it and then remained in silence for a moment until one man said, "I think God wants us to do thus and so," and another said, "Yes, and then we are supposed to do such and such." And thus a plan evolved.

As we begin to work out our idea in action, we find that our human equipment is functioning at its very best. Indeed, we often find ourselves "playing over our head," doing better than we could have hoped to do because God has freed us to become the persons He created us to be. And in the matter of physical and worldly equipment for our project, until you have tried this, you will find it difficult to believe how things are available as they are needed if we have faith that God is in command. Anyone who has ever built a mission church with little funds will have seen how God meets recurring crises with just the right dollar or just the right donated material at the exact crucial moment when all progress is ready to stop.

As to drive or the resolution to see the thing through, if God be for us, who can be against us? We press on firmly because we have committed the whole thing to the One Who is going to be with us every step of the way. And as for luck, we Christians call it divine providence. We cannot possibly foresee the myriad crossroads and pathways and obstacles that lie before our project. But God can, and we find ourselves arriving at the right time at the right place. Each needed thing falls into place exactly as it is needed. Doors open before us as we go, and if a door closes somewhere, God opens a window that we can go through. Things work out until, in the end, people look at what has happened and say, "It's a miracle!"

Let me tell you, beloved, whatever you have to do, if you do it in the power of God, you are likely to see a miracle.

# CHAPTER SEVENTEEN

## *PROPHECY*

"Lord, speak to me that I may speak,
In living echoes of thy tone.
As thou hast sought so let me seek,
Thy erring children, lost and lone.
O teach me Lord, that I may teach,
The precious things thou dost impart.
And wing my words, that they may reach
The hidden depths of many a heart."

Hymn 574, *The Hymnal 1940*

When we let the Lord speak through us, we are exercising the gift of prophecy. This is one of the power gifts, and it is one of the vocal gifts that children of God receive when they yield control of their lives to Him through Christ.

These are called ministry gifts because they are given us to profit by, to make use of, to minister with for the benefit of the fellowship. The gift of prophecy may be seen in other people that you know in the Christian fold, or it may come to you. It is therefore good to know all you can about it.

The first thing to emphasize about the gift of prophecy is that it is a gift; it comes from God and it does not depend upon your own intellectual powers. Any true Christian prophecy may be prefaced with the words, "Thus said the Lord . . ."

A member of our Spanish congregation at Holy Comforter Church in Miami awoke one Sunday morning with a strong urge to write something. She arose, got pen and paper, and began to put down the words that came to her. She covered more than a page with closely spaced writing. She brought what she had written to Father Valdes, our fine Spanish priest, and when he had read it, he said, "I think God means this for the congregation to hear." So he read it to the people at the Spanish-language service that Sunday. It was a message couched in terms and written in phrases far above the simple talents of the woman who had brought it. Father Valdes told his people that he believed this was a message from God. Thirty minutes after the service, a woman came to him as he was preparing to leave the church and said, "I came to your service today for the first time. I do not know why I came, but the message was for me. I have already gone and attended to the matter it referred to, and my whole life has been changed. Thank you." But Father Valdes thanked the obedient person who had written down the prophecy God gave her.

The second thing about prophecy is true precisely because it is a gift from God, and that is that it must be accepted or received. God does not force any of His gifts upon us; three qualifications for receiving a gift of God are necessary.

These qualifications are that we have faith that we can receive such a gift, that we be open and willing to accept it, and that we take an initial step in faith.

Our faith that we can receive such a gift may be based simply upon the Bible evidence. It can also be strengthened by what we see going on among other Christians. If you are in a group in which prophecies are being received and uttered, it will be much easier for you to believe that you too can receive one.

The second two qualifications go together. If you are truly open to be used as a channel of God's grace, then you will put up no bars to that grace flowing through you. And it seems as if God, in His desire not to force Himself on us, requires us not only to be willing, but to take the first step.

Let me illustrate like this: If you are in meditation and hold yourself ready to receive a prophecy from God, you may receive the bare glimmering of an idea, the first words, perhaps, of a message from on high. Until you speak these words out in faith, often you will not receive the next words that are to come. This sort of launching out in faith upon something that requires God to move in immediately to hold you up, is typical of the ministry gifts. Often when I sit down to write of the things of God, I have no idea what God wants me to say beyond the first paragraph. But I write that in faith, and the rest begins to come.

Now, what is prophecy? If we believe that it comes from God, then we must believe that it contains something that God wants said. The material that it contains may have to do with the past, the present, or the future. Unfortunately, the word "prophecy" just now in our society is being used to refer almost exclusively to the future.

Some prophecy is of this nature. I think it is a mistake to classify all supernatural revelation of the future as demonic. Certainly there are evil forces in the world which can guide fortune-tellers, necromancers, seers, and soothsayers. But God has revealed His plans in advance to His people many times in history. I'm sure He still does so. Of course, it is quite possible for humans to misuse natural gifts as they do every other God-given ability.

Usually when God tells us that something is going to happen, He uses our mental faculties. In other words, we "get an idea." If this idea comes as we are in prayer and seeking God's guidance, then we should be very careful to treat it as something divinely inspired. This means that we test it against what experience and scripture have told us about God, and then we seek to find what God wants us to do about the idea. If it is His will that we proclaim to others whatever has been revealed to us, then this is called prophecy.

Quite often, it is more important to tell it forth than for it to be foretelling. A prophetic utterance may deal with future consequences of present acts and may need to be proclaimed that all may know where a course may lead. Such an utterance may need only a minimum of divine inspiration if the facts are plain enough.

The reason that we do not hear more prophecy in the world today is that people are too reluctant to speak out. He who stands forth as a prophet risks suffering the fate of a prophet, which in this life may not be at all pleasant. But if your prayer life leads you to something that God wants you to share with others, your choice is obedience or disobedience.

Those of us who are preachers seek professionally for God's guidance in order that we may share with you, not just our own words, but His. But how glorious it would be if all of God's people allowed Him to use them to speak through. If done humbly rather than just proclaiming one's own opinion, such telling represents a sharing of revelation, and the world is richer for it.

Our world would be quite different if we all were obedient to the heavenly vision. In your prayer life, let God speak to you, and then consider very carefully as He does speak that He may wish what He gives you to be passed on to others.

# CHAPTER EIGHTEEN

## *DISCERNMENT*

One of the abilities which we can have as Spirit-filled Christians is the ability to distinguish between spirits. The King James Version of the Bible calls this discerning of spirits. The Revised Standard Version refers to it as an ability to distinguish between them. A discerning person is usually thought of as one who knows what he is about, who makes good value judgments of the things which affect his life, and acts accordingly.

Insofar as we might be speaking here about telling the difference between good and bad, this might be thought to be no more than the usual concept that the man in the street has of religion, i.e., that the purpose of religion is to teach human beings the difference between right and wrong, and to reward or punish them according to their conduct. Rather primitive this, but a widely held view. Hence the common saying, "I'm just as good as those who go to church," which implies that this is what one goes for.

There is no question but what those who live in Christ exhibit a different moral quality in their lives than those who do not. "By their fruits shall ye know them." But this is not because they are honor students in a religious school which has taught them better than most which is the proper course to follow. The sanctions of religion, heaven, and hell, have not proven to be very effective ways of motivating people. Social pressures, the wish to conform, and police power have had far more effect on human conduct than the threat of a burning hell if you remain a sinner, or the promise of heaven if you are good. One could rest this case on the number of people who do something about their religion on any given Sunday morning.

In these days of situation ethics, when we are being told that the rightness or wrongness of a thing does not rest in the thing itself but in the total situation, many are confused as to just what is good and what is bad, what is right (for them) and wrong. The Christian has two things going for him — an eternal standard of things that are right and wrong, and a Judge and Adviser Who goes with him everywhere to give on-the-spot advice on doubtful situations. To say that it all depends on the situation, really means that it all depends on you. Human beings do not measure up well to this kind of responsibility. But if the rule books have been thrown away, how nice it is to go everywhere in company with the Author of the books.

Much more is involved here than making value judgments about situations and actions, much more indeed. Those who would reduce Christianity to a species of legalism in which it is only necessary to learn God's law and then follow it, are not very well acquainted with mankind. We do not keep the law simply by virtue of knowing what it is. We have to be motivated toward the law, and we are quite likely to be motivated in the opposite direction.

Our motivation, that which makes us do what we do, comes from two sources. There is that inner drive which seeks the satisfaction of our appetites, our goals. And there is that which influences us from without, that would have us move in directions which are perhaps contrary to what we might otherwise choose. How often have you been in a situation in which "something tells you" to follow a certain course of action? This can be much more than an educated conscience. This can be an outside source of guidance and motivation. We are concerned in this chapter with these outside influences.

Christians have believed from the beginning in evil spirits, sometimes called demons. Christ sent His disciples forth to cast them out in His name. And they met with success. When

I was a boy, I thought that the idea of evil spirits was just a superstition that the ancients had because they did not understand the true nature of sickness and mental illness and human perversity. There's nothing like twenty years experience as a pastor to teach one how vital are the forces which work upon people from without. Perhaps we have a semantic or language difficulty, but I now find no problem at all in thinking of these forces as spiritual, as having being, and as possessing considerable power.

We are in a realm here in which manifestations range from the very subtle to the overwhelming. God Himself often speaks to us in a still small voice, while the surging temptation to murder, bodily lust, or addiction to drugs or alcohol screams in the hearts and minds of those who are its prey. If these outside influences, however they may manifest themselves, would only wear plainly marked labels, man would at least be able to make an intelligent choice. But the voice that whispers in your mind that a certain course of conduct is desirable is not always clearly identifiable, and thus the easiest thing is simply to consider it your own voice and to go ahead and do whatever it makes you want to do. This is the cult of doing what you feel like doing; some would call it freedom, but it often brings pain to someone else.

Let us assume that you are a person who is kindly disposed toward the world and who is willing, within reason, to set aside your own desires if their satisfaction would cause harm to anyone. Given the very common definition that what is good will satisfy you without hurting anyone else and what is bad will hurt people, possibly including yourself, what is a man to do? How can he know?

One of the first things you can do is to test the spirit that seeks to guide you. You can test what is being suggested against what you know of human law and immutable divine law. If murder, for example, is what is being suggested, you can be certain that the spirit is evil that suggests it. Next lift up the suggested course of action in prayer. Is this something that God will bless and prosper? The very thought of praying about it may be enough to show you that it doesn't fit what you know of God's will for you.

If you are filled with the Spirit of God, if Christ is living in your heart, then you have a special ability to discern or distinguish between spirits. When you meet another person, if he is filled with the love of Christ, that same love in you will immediately warm to His presence, and you will know that you have met a comrade. We are often asked how Spirit-filled people find one another in our complex society. The answer lies in the gift of discerning of spirits; you can discern a good spirit just as quickly as a bad one.

If you come face-to-face with a person or a situation in which the power of Satan is at work, you know this, too. There is that within you, there is that One within you, who responds to the presence of evil in a way that you will recognize. Some Christians have this gift more highly developed than others and can be of great use to the fellowship in locating and identifying antagonistic forces that need to be driven out by the power of Christ.

I know a lady in a southern town who is particularly acute in this regard. Those who are troubled by the presence in their lives of something that persistently tries to lead them away from God's will, can come to this woman and find help in identifying the particular seat of the problem so that they can pray more intelligently about it. Although it is possible to magnify Satan's power by overemphasis on these things, it is often helpful to have the guidance of one who has the gift of discerning of spirits highly developed. All Christians can have this gift in some degree.

Thus one who is indwelt by the Spirit of God comes to know that there are principalities and powers that would make of your life something other than what God wants made. And so he tests every spirit; he places every situation before the throne of grace so that God's sweet light can shine into all the dark places; and then, in God's power, he banishes the evil, and sets forth to follow the good, moving out on his journey of faith toward the destiny that God's love has prepared for him.

# CHAPTER NINETEEN

## *TONGUES AND INTERPRETATION*

Two of the gifts of the Spirit listed in I Corinthians 12 are tongues and interpretation of tongues. Paul goes on in Chapter 14 to give a great deal of attention to these two gifts, their use and their dangers. None of the other gifts in the list of nine receives anything like this amount of emphasis. In the same manner today, speaking in tongues and the interpretation that sometimes follows are receiving vastly more attention than the other gifts. The result is that the revival of interest in the power of the Holy Spirit is often known as the "tongues movement," and some of its devotees lay stress upon tongues almost to the exclusion of the other gifts.

We are seeking to deal in this book with a fairly wide range of experiences which come to those who yield their lives to Christ and are filled with His Holy Spirit. Speaking in tongues is just one of these experiences. We believe with Paul that all of these manifestations are given to us to profit by and that it is extremely dangerous to the spiritual well-being of an individual to focus on one gift to the extent that interest in others is diminished.

Speaking in tongues, strange phenomenon that it is, is real and is a part of the whole package of gifts which come to us from God. It has some important values that we want to deal with. We should no more set this gift aside because it is sometimes misunderstood or misused than we should shun the gifts of healing or discerning of spirits just because they are sometimes misused by charlatans. In our experience, most spiritual leaders who are open to whatever gifts God wants them to have, eventually receive the gift of tongues. Not all talk about it; there is a definite stigma attached to it in many quarters; but we are no longer surprised to hear that this person or that person of national prominence has received, in addition to other spiritual gifts, the gift of tongues.

Speaking in tongues has a mechanical and a spiritual side. On the mechanical side, it involves the entire speech mechanism — tongue, teeth, lips, palate, vocal cords, lungs, etc. But it does not involve the conscious mind, except that the mind must be willing for the physical body to manifest this gift. Speaking in tongues is voluntary, that is, you can start and stop at will. But the actual control of what is said, the tone, the shaping of the syllables, the phrasing, etc., is not done at the conscious direction of the speaker.

Many of us have come to believe that God uses our subconscious minds to manifest this gift. It would be possible, if there were any point to it, for a person to do arithmetical problems in his conscious mind while continuing to pray in tongues. Therefore, we say that control of the speech mechanism is vested somewhere other than in the conscious mind.

The resulting speech is not mere gibberish or an uncontrolled series of random sounds. It is inflected, emphasized, divided into sentences and phrases; quite often it is sublimely beautiful to hear. It is far removed from the ravings of an idiot, and it is quite different from the nonsense of someone who might attempt to mock the gift or to simulate its possession.

Our main interest is in the spiritual aspects of this gift. First and foremost, speaking in tongues involves a very complete yielding of self to God. Our speech mechanism involves the highest cortical centers of the brain, and yielding those to divine control does away with the mental reservations with which we are apt to hedge about many of our surrenders to God. Speaking in tongues involves not only a spiritual yielding, but also a mental and a physical surrender. Bypassing the conscious mind as it does, tongues-speaking gives you no opportunity to consider each syllable given you by God before you speak it out. You can no longer retain the veto power which keeps much spiritual yielding from being truly total.

This sort of trust is basic to the operation of all the gifts. More than this, there is a required initiative on your part to make the gift manifest. Just as Peter did not walk on the water until he got himself out of the boat at Jesus' command, so no one speaks in tongues until he is willing to begin to speak. I have seen people deep in silent prayer, waiting for God to speak through their mouths. But it doesn't work this way. You begin to speak, to make sounds of praise, and God immediately begins to shape and form them. The same thing is true with all the gifts. God offers the gift, you respond in faith by making a start, and then the gift comes. It is like proclaiming a prophecy of which God has given you only the first line; when you have spoken out that first line, the second comes. Speaking in tongues requires that you receive guidance from God second by second, syllable by syllable. It is an excellent spiritual exercise in being open to what God has to give, as well as a useful means of praise and adoration.

We cannot do anything that is pleasing to God without His help. Certainly when we pray, we ought to pray first for help in praying. There are prayers of petition in which we really do not know what God would have us ask. We can make these in the new language God gives us. There are prayers of thanksgiving in which we do not know how to thank God adequately for His many blessings. We can do the best we know how and then let His Spirit guide the rest of our thanks.

But it is in the realm of praise that the heavenly language is most obviously useful, for it is in praise that we are most obviously deficient in our own abilities.

It is a rare person who can praise God for five minutes in his own words. Praise is the most unselfish of all kinds of prayer. Thanksgiving is not praise; it is an expression of gratitude for *our* blessings. Confession deals with our sins, intercession with the needs of our friends, and petition with our personal needs. But praise tells God how wonderful He is and how much we love Him just because He is Who He is. If it were not for the great words of praise that have come down to us through the centuries, we would be speechless before the majesty of God. But after using the words of others and our own halting words of praise, how great it is to let God's Holy Spirit take our voice and raise it in praise of Him in a heavenly language.

We can testify that prayer burdens that could not be lifted up with any other form of prayer are lifted instantly when we offer them in the language God gives. We can testify to the utility of having an extra prayer language as we come to situation after situation in which we know not what to pray for. One grieving wife wanted me to pray for the restoration of her husband's sight as he lay in a hospital bed, heavily bandaged after an auto accident. I knew that his eye had already been removed, and although I didn't know exactly what prayer thoughts to lift up to God, I pictured him well and whole, and prayed quietly in the Spirit. God did not heal his body, but after the man had time to straighten out several relationship problems with friends and family, he joined our Lord. This experience of letting God teach me what to say, has occurred many times in my ministry, in English as well as in tongues.

Once you have yielded your speech mechanisms to God and have learned to manifest whatever speech the Holy Spirit gives you, a whole new world of prayer opens up. While most people seem to have a basic language, these languages differ as much as the fingerprints of those who speak them. And from time to time, we receive new languages. We find ourselves praying in a tongue quite different from that which we ordinarily use, and we give thanks for this renewed evidence of the presence of God in our prayer life. Sometimes a person will speak out in a known language, one he has never learned. When this happens, it is not unusual for a person who knows this earthly language to translate what is said. This is one of God's miracles, and it happens more frequently than one might imagine.

We have been speaking of tongues as a form of prayer. The gift also appears as a form of prophecy or speaking out in God's name. On occasion when Spirit-filled people are praying and worshiping together, someone in the company may be impelled to speak aloud in a tongue, in order that what they say may be heard by others. When this happens, it is customary for the group to pause until the speaker or someone else present receives an interpretation of what is said. This interpretation is also a spiritual gift, and it comes to the conscious mind of someone who is willing to speak it out. He may receive only the first few words of the interpretation, but when he begins speaking out in faith, the rest will come.

The word of the Lord as it comes in this way is usually in the first person, is sometimes in the words of holy scripture, and often consists of encouragement or exhortation for the members of the group. It is an interpretation rather than a translation of the God-given language. On one occasion we heard a message given in French by someone who knew no French. Someone in the crowd of more than a thousand people present that day gave the interpretation. He did not know French either. Then someone who did know French, congratulated the original speaker on his accent and gave a literal translation. The interpretation and the translation were markedly similar, but one dealt with literal word-for-word translation into English and the other gave the broad meaning of the whole passage in spiritual terms.

By far the vast majority of those who speak in tongues do so in private prayer, and this is, of course, their own private concern. Paul spoke of the dangers of public utterances in a tongue unknown to the group, and these dangers still exist. In some groups there are people who will speak out in a tongue in order to draw attention to themselves. This places them in great spiritual danger and does not edify the rest of the group. This is sometimes referred to as being "in the flesh." But when a group is in the Spirit and a message comes, its beauty and the significance of the interpretation that follows are easily understood to be of God. Sometimes in a group there will be singing in the Spirit. This is a heavenly harmony in which people in prayer sing such notes and enunciate such syllables as they are led to do. It is never planned and never led, except by the Spirit. The result is a harmony unlike anything heard elsewhere on this earth, and once heard, never forgotten.

The gifts of the Spirit are given us to profit by. As we receive them and manifest them, so is God glorified and His work done in our lives and in the fields He has given us to harvest.

# CHAPTER TWENTY

## *THE MARKS OF THE SPIRIT*

Not long ago, my daughter threw away a fall or wig that she had grown tired of, and I picked it up and decided to have some fun with it. Putting it on my nearly bald head, I also put a brightly colored shirt over my clerical shirt and turned-around collar, donned some love beads and a large medallion on a gold chain, put on some dark glasses, and sallied forth to attend a meeting of a couples' club of our church.

When I entered the home where this rather lively group was meeting, I was immediately recognized by those who knew me well. But the visitors at the gathering saw nothing of the balding cleric they had heard about in this hairy figure spouting hippie talk, and they did not know me at all. We may suppose, however, that even had I not resumed my normal garb later in the evening, they would soon have come to see another part of me as the events of the evening went on. My point, of course, is that not only does God see beneath the surface of a person, but so do other people. That which is inside will make itself evident sooner or later.

We are well able to wear masks in the society in which we live today because, except in small towns, we move in quite separate circles of people, some of whom we know at work, some at play, some at church, and very, very few in more than one part of our lives. It is therefore possible to act like a Christian with people whom you do not know well and get away with it. This can happen even within the church fellowship to some extent. But it does not prove that all who profess and call themselves Christians are indeed good

Christians, but only that they are good actors. As old as the Sabbath is the accusation that some people are religious only one day a week. Their act is not permanent, because it is only an act, not something welling up from within.

The fruits of the Spirit can be counterfeited by one who is willing to act out the features of a good character. But there are evidences of a Spirit-filled life which are not so easily counterfeited, things which are the result of a changed life. This final section of our book deals with them. We have a neat list in I Corinthians 12 of the gifts of the Spirit and in Galatians 5 of the fruits of the Spirit. Now here, in the Gospel according to Hall, if you'll pardon me, we offer a list of the marks of the Spirit or the evidences of the Spirit.

These are the things which we have observed over the years to be typical of the life of a Spirit-filled person. We have had the glorious experience of watching the power of Jesus Christ begin to be manifested in the lives of hundreds of newly reborn Christians in that time, and one by one these marks of that infilling have appeared. We had planned to list nine of them in order to make a neat package with the nine gifts and the nine fruits, but the Holy Spirit refuses to be packaged, and we found that we wanted to tell about eleven of them. There are, of course, many more. But those who are in a Spirit-filled fellowship will recognize the picture we are painting.

The fruits of the Spirit have to do with character, with the changed inner being of one who is taken over by the Spirit of Christ. The gifts of the Spirit have to do with power, with the supernatural helps given to one through whom Christ has begun to minister to the world. The marks of the Spirit describe those changes in a Spirit-filled person which have to do with his life-style, his way of life. He is different, not only in what he is, but in what he does, and in what he is now able to do. Because he is different, the world reacts to him differently, and so his environment changes as he changes. This environment includes other people and other spiritual powers, and the way he relates to them is part of his new life.

I don't think the marks of the Spirit are something that anyone can or would particularly want to copy. They are just things that happen when your life-style changes. They are not goals to be sought so much as things that you will note when it happens to you, too. I tell you now so that when the time comes, you will remember that I told you of them. And since God's providence is incredibly beautiful, when you have come to know all of these things, never fear, there's more.

# CHAPTER TWENTY-ONE

## *MORE BIBLE*

One of the things that quickly becomes apparent in the life of a Spirit-filled person is a new love for the Holy Bible. This is not due to conformity to what one thinks he ought to do, but to a genuine hunger for the word of God as it is revealed in the pages of scripture.

There are so many misconceptions about the Bible that it is difficult to discuss reading it without attempting to correct some of these things. Perhaps it would be sufficient to say that many of us need a new approach to the Bible; we read it in such special ways and with such special attitudes that our minds are sometimes closed to what God has to say to us.

The divisions of the Bible into chapter and verse, for example, are convenient for study and analysis, but place a rather artificial structure upon it. What else do we read, unless it be civil law, which is so codified and broken up? In like manner, the Bible is such a special book that we surround the reading of it with a sort of aura which removes it from the rest of our daily existence.

You can read the Bible, of course, without being a religious person at all. The Bible can be read as literature, as history, and as poetry. Some parts rank very high in these categories. But considered in this light, the Bibles of the world would gather vastly more dust than they do if they were read only for secular purposes.

The importance of the Bible is that it contains the word of God. I like to make this distinction rather than saying that the Bible is the Word of God. I recognize that one Christian viewpoint considers every word in the Bible to have come direct from the throne of heaven. But another view is that the Bible is in the words of men. God inspired these men, and therefore what they wrote contains the word of God. But it also contains some very human mistakes and misquotes that I should dislike to attribute to God. The Bible contains all things necessary to salvation. But that is not the same thing as saying that you must believe everything in the Bible to be saved.

More important than what the Bible says, is what God says to you while you are reading it. Reading the Bible with God's Holy Spirit illuminating your mind is a new experience of communication with God. For as you read these words set down so many centuries ago, God speaks to your needs of today with a clear guidance and inspiration that contributes mightily to your Christian growth.

You can miss this if you immerse yourself too deeply in the proof-text way of reading. By this I mean the system that collects individual verses under every conceivable heading and presents them to you for guidance whenever a situation under that particular heading comes along. Texts such as "Love thy neighbor," "Turn the other cheek," and "Go and sin no more" contain truth. But truth removed from its context or background may not be as meaningful. There is the old chestnut about taking Bible verses out of context which uses "Judas went into the garden and hanged himself," and "Go thou and do likewise." This is silly, of course, but it points to a danger in isolating texts. Someone has said that a text out of context is a pretext.

But for the Spirit-filled person, our point is not that the method of Bible reading is so important as is our attitude while we do it. If we take the Bible as a reference book, then we will skim through its pages looking for a situation similar to the one we are in, in order to see what God did about it two thousand or more years ago. I find it is more practical to turn the situation over to God to do with as He pleases, and then simply to read the Bible by almost any system and be open to what God wants to tell you. You will find to your surprise that certain passages just leap out at you. You will find that you are reading exactly what you need to read because God will put into your mind and heart those ideas and desires that He wants there as you immerse yourself in holy scripture. The contrast is almost that between saying, "Lord, you tell me what to do, and in the meantime, I'll read the Bible," and "Lord, don't worry about a thing; I'm going to take my Bible and figure this matter out myself." It is really the difference between using the Bible as a reference book by your human ability and using the Bible as a point of contact between you and your God in order that He may give you your marching orders.

This is not to say that we should not study the Bible, that we should not steep ourselves in its stories, in the history of God's dealings with men, with the story of our Lord and of the early church. Not at all. But to do that by itself is not enough. A secular person could do the same. Our plea here is based on our observation of the ways God feeds those who turn to Him for feeding. And the Holy Bible is one of the main channels through which spiritual nourishment comes.

The Bible means far more to you after you are converted than it does before. The Bible is much used in evangelism as a tool for conversion. We hear of those who have been converted by reading just one Gospel, or even by pondering the meaning of just one verse. This is wonderful. But we have seen a lot of people converted to a deeply meaningful life in the Spirit, and it seems important to emphasize that the Bible is a tool or an agent in such conversions, not the cause of them.

If this be the case, then it is vitally important to use the Bible as the channel that God intends it to be. It's all very well to ask which comes first, conversion or meaningful Bible reading, but in actual practice, the Bible isn't very much good until the reader or hearer has some motivation really to listen to what God is saying through its words. To quote scripture and underline its claims on the basis that it is God's word is meaningless to someone who does not even believe in God. This is the logical fallacy of arguing in a circle, of using the thing you are trying to prove to prove itself.

But let there be a spark of interest, no matter how tiny, in the heart of an inquirer; let him take only the smallest step of faith; and the Bible speaks well and truly to him. When one's heart is full of the Spirit of God, the Bible speaks in a great flood of God's love and goodness and uplifting presence.

Undoubtedly, those who love the Lord, love His book. But we would counsel that inquirers be shown God at work in the world today as well as the record of what He said and did thousands of years ago. Jesus Christ is the same yesterday, today, and forever, but those who have not yet met Him must do so first in the present, and then they can appreciate the eternal truths enunciated in the past.

As you come to know Jesus well, as His power fills your life throughout each day, you come to feel a great kinship for those who have gone before. Just as you are hungry for fellowship with others who are children of His Spirit in this century, so you can come to know and understand those of olden times who knew the same loving God in their day. To know Him better, you must read your Bible. And as you know Him better, you will hunger for His word. It is there for you in the pages of the book He inspired.

# CHAPTER TWENTY-TWO

## *MORE PRAYER*

Those of us who belong to the great liturgical churches have a richness in our public prayer life because of the prayers developed and handed down by the church through the centuries. Those prayers which best express man's religious aspirations have endured, and those which were not so apt have disappeared. We can find in our books of prayers a suitable petition or thanksgiving or word of praise for almost any public occasion.

But when it comes time to talk to God in the privacy of our own prayer closet, wherever that may be, we find that we are dependent still upon the printed page. We are somehow inarticulate when it comes to expressing our deepest feelings and needs in our own words. This is even more true if we are asked to lead others in prayer. Here we almost always turn to written prayers.

Now for one who wants to live very close to God and to be in constant communication with Him, this dependence upon written prayer is stifling. And for one who is called to work with groups and frequently to lead them in prayer, this reliance on the book is awkward, to say the least. And obviously, the more personal and private the prayer subject, the less likely one is to find the exact expression of it in a book. You can spend your whole prayer time leafing through devotional books, seeking just the right prayer to say exactly what you want to say. We know people who do this.

But cheer up, there's more. There's more power to pray for those who yield their lives to God in Christ. Those who are filled with the Spirit receive the ability to pray extemporaneously and freely and quite often beautifully. For many, the ability is given in an instant. One moment you cannot pray without a book, and the next moment you can talk to God all day and all night if you wish, freely and openly. You can lead prayer for others without embarrassment, and you find words and phrases coming to your lips that surprise even you, for you did not consciously think of them. There seems to be a connection between this ability and the yielding of your speech mechanisms in tongues or prophecy. Obviously, if you learn to let God speak through your mouth in an unknown language, He can do it in one that you know.

The inspiration of the Holy Spirit is not an empty phrase. Men and women down through the centuries have found themselves bringing forth ideas for which they themselves are not truly responsible. Without going into a deep psychological discussion, most of us are aware that we have a conscious and a subconscious or unconscious mind. This subconscious of ours is the repository of everything we have ever experienced. Many things that we cannot reach consciously are still there below the surface, and they have their effect on us.

When God deals with the whole man, when we yield every bit of our life, body, mind, and spirit, to Him, then He deals with us on levels other than the purely conscious mental level on which most people would like to keep Him. God deals with the person who is filled with His Spirit in bodily ways, in spiritual ways, and on every level of the mind. Thus many things happen that might seem inexplicable on the conscious level. They do not contradict what we know of God's laws; they simply use material not ordinarily available to us.

There is a written prayer that says, "Oh God, forasmuch as without thee we cannot do anything that will please thee, mercifully grant that by the inspiration of thy Holy Spirit, we may . . ." There is a profound truth there. Of course we want our prayer expressions to be pleasing to God. Of course we want Him to find our praise and our thanksgiving couched in exactly the proper terms. We cannot hope to do this without His help. But if we are filled with His Spirit, if we yield every possible facet of our life to Him, then we cannot do anything without being guided by Him. And insofar as we let Him inspire our prayers, just so far will our prayers be truly pleasing to Him. Before I came into this closer walk with God, my extemporaneous prayers were halting and consisted mostly of learned phrases from familiar prayers. Almost overnight, it seemed, I could go along an altar rail filled with people, ask each one for what he wished me to pray, and then compose fresh prayers on the spot.

One mark of Spirit-filled prayer is the frequent faint sense of amazement you feel as you find yourself praying in words that you have not first thought about. We are taught from early childhood to think before we speak, and when we speak out in prayer in words that we find strange to our conscious minds, it is startling. But one soon learns to accept gratefully this precious gift. You soon learn not to prepare a prayer to say, but to prepare yourself to pray. If you are asked to lead in prayer, you don't rush for a book; you simply become quiet inside and ask God to lead you as you lead the others. In many churches, the minister does this formally in the ritual as he begins prayer. He asks the Lord to be with the congregation that is going to pray together, and the congregation prays that the Lord will inspire the minister. Then they pray. In Latin or English it goes like this:

Minister: The Lord be with you.

People: And with your spirit. (Or, And also with you.)

Minister: Let us pray.

As with all spiritual gifts, the gift of extemporaneous prayer must be accepted by the recipient. God does not force any of His gifts upon us. It seems as if He offers them, holds them out to us, to take or to ignore according to our own will. Receiving spiritual gifts requires faith, and as we point out in the chapter on faith, this itself is a gift. Receiving the gift of extemporaneous prayer requires launching out in faith. Just as the disciples, who had toiled all night without taking a single fish, went back out and let down their nets another time when Jesus told them to, so we who would pray aloud by the inspiration of God begin to do so by beginning. No matter how tongue-tied we have been in the past, if we want God's power in this matter, we must make a start. Without having any idea of what we are going to say, we begin to pray aloud.

We can at least say, "Dear God," or "Oh, Heavenly Father," or make some other form of address. Immediately other words will come to you. If it is only one word, say it out in faith that another will follow instantly. If you do not launch forth in faith, the next words will not come. The gift is there, but you must seize it, use it, accept it. And as you pray these words trustingly, you become more and more open to the inspiration of the Holy Spirit, so that the words do not come haltingly, but freely and wonderfully, until you feel like stopping your prayer just to praise and thank God for the gift of being able to pray.

The next breath you are going to take is a gift of God. If He withholds His hand, you will not take it. How seldom do we realize the gifts of God that are woven intimately into our lives. How gratefully we can thank Him as we let Him guide our hearts and minds in prayer. How gloriously can we praise Him as we realize just Who and what He is.

This gift of prayer will change your life still more. Prayer is one of the basic methods by which God speaks to you, teaches you, inspires you, empowers you. You will learn to listen as well as to speak; you will learn to spend time being open to God's transmissions into your life. Where once you read a few prayers out of a sense of duty, now you will find yourself resenting the end of your prayer time. But God has work for you to do in the world. Your prayer time is your visit to headquarters to get your instructions, to draw your equipment for the tasks that lie before you. And then you go out, knowing that you can speak to God and that He can speak to you, wherever you may be, in quiet or in tumult, in public or in private, in happiness or in sorrow, for He has given through His Holy Spirit the gift of prayer to one who was ready to receive it.

# CHAPTER TWENTY-THREE

## *MORE SACRIFICE*

One of the basic tenets of the Christian religion is self-sacrifice. "He who loses his life shall find it," is the paradox at the heart of everything we believe in. It should be no surprise to anyone that the founder of our faith, Jesus Christ, practiced self-sacrifice right up to and including His own death. And by losing His life, He found it; for God raised Him up from the dead; death hath no more dominion over Him.

Knowing that in any large group of church people, half will be unconverted, I am bound to say that for those who have not truly surrendered their lives to God through Christ, all this talk of self-sacrifice sounds a good bit like nonsense. Paul referred to the crucifixion as a stumbling block to the Jews; they simply could not understand the Messiah allowing Himself to be treated like this.

It is very difficult for a selfish person to accept the idea of self-sacrifice as a total way of life. I am a selfish person, so I can speak with authority on this. We want to measure out our self-sacrifice in small doses, carefully calculated to do us no harm, and sometimes calculated just as carefully to get us a maximum of publicity, or if not that, then a maximum of personal satisfaction. And when we do this, we miss the point.

One can scarcely announce to someone, "I am now going to do something that I find quite unpleasant, but I'm going to do it because I love you." Whatever this deed may be, it isn't going to turn out to be self-sacrifice, because the person has already milked the situation for every bit of martyred glory that he can get out of it.

We live in a world whose motto is "What's in it for me?" As long as our citizenship is in this world, we will never understand conduct the result of which is an apparent net loss for me. Of course I might miss a meal and send the money I save to starving people in Africa, especially if I can do this in company with others so that we can reassure ourselves about what good fellows we are. That's the way of this world. But try doing it without telling anyone.

You might want to point out that when Jesus hung on the cross, He had plenty of publicity. True enough, but the very kind of jeering, humiliating attention that He got, was a part of the sacrifice. He gave not only His life, He offered up not only blood and pain, but also His tears. He was shamed and spat upon; no bugles blew for Him; no bands played a glorious victory march for the martyred leader. The whole event smelled of defeat.

If you yield the control of your life to the risen Christ, if He is in control instead of you, you will find yourself called to do things just as ridiculous as He did, ridiculous in the sight of the world. And the world will often let you hear its ridicule.

I want you to face the fact that there are many people who join the church and engage in good works without knowing the Christ or yielding to Him. I want you to consider that you may be one of these people. Religion is under fire in many quarters today, but it is still quite popular to belong to a church and to do good things. I have nothing against doing good things, but it makes an eternal difference as to what your reason is for doing them. You receive no credit in heaven for good deeds if you do them for your own benefit, your own pleasure, your own public profit. Think about this.

Jesus died on the cross willingly and freely. He could have avoided this final act; He could have sidestepped neatly as He had done before. He Who was without sin did not deserve to die as a sinful man; He paid the price of sin willingly so that we wouldn't have to. Despite the sorrow and shame of His death, despite His human repugnance for this kind of death as showed in the scene in the garden, it is not too much to say that Jesus died gladly; His last word was a shout of triumph.

The kind of self-sacrifice which we are led to in this world will contain the same elements of quiet joy, of willingness to spend and be spent in His service. The reason for this is not hard to find. God is love, and those who give themselves to Him are filled with the Spirit of love. Love is always self-sacrificing; love always seeks the good of the loved one.

As a church leader of some experience, I have seen all sorts of people doing church work. Some of them are committed to the organization, some enjoy being useful in company with others, some are seeking either personal or public recognition of their gift of time and energy. But quite different is the worker who has sacrificed his life to the Lord. In practice, he may be apparently only subtly different from those who are doing the same work, but he is engaged in a deeper level of effort. Those who are only "doing their duty" do not take kindly to unscheduled calls for help; self-sacrificing Christians do. They have only to be shown a need to begin to respond.

You cannot live a Spirit-filled life in this world without being moved with compassion for those whom the Father creates and loves. As the love of God fills your heart, you find yourself doing perfectly outrageous things for these people with no thought of how ridiculous this might seem to others. "What's in it for me?" – the question just doesn't occur to you.

I'm not speaking here of the planned good works of organized religion. I'm speaking of the fruits, the manifestations of the gifts in the ministry of a yielded Christian. Jesus says, "As my Father has sent me, even so send I you." And it is our glad task to go, wherever it may be. One of the first things I noticed about Spirit-filled Christians was their willingness to go. I could call one of them at three in the morning and say that someone needed help, and they would simply ask for the address so that they could get up and go.

More self-sacrifice may seem a stumbling block to the Jews and foolishness to the gentiles, but the more you live your life in Him, the more you lose your life in Him, the more will He give it to you, good measure, pressed down, and running over — the hallmark of the truly abundant life.

# CHAPTER TWENTY-FOUR

## *MORE WITNESSING*

Jesus said, "Ye shall receive power, after that the Holy Ghost is come upon you. And ye shall be witnesses unto me." Of all the things of which there is more for the person who yields fully and completely, a greatly increased ability to witness is a quality to be seen in many. Jesus promised power for this, and He makes good His promise for all who are willing to receive it.

The word "witness" as a verb is not particularly popular in some church circles. We think of a witness as a person who has been present at a happening and who has a special knowledge because of this. We are more likely to refer to his description of what he has seen as his "testimony" rather than as his witness. But we find a considerable reluctance among church people to give their Christian testimony too, so perhaps we'd better back off and just use the word that Jesus used, translated into modern English, as best we can.

Now to give a witness requires first of all that you have witnessed or seen something. Secondly, it requires that you have an audience. Thirdly, it requires that you be willing and able to bear witness. Jesus said that when we are filled with the Holy Spirit, we will witness. And we find in fact that the willingness to be used of Him in any way He chooses, includes the willingness to witness. When we offer ourselves in this way, He graciously provides us with the other three essentials; namely, an experience about which to witness, an audience to whom to witness, and the words with which to give the witness.

This is what we call a "package deal" – we get the whole

thing at once. It sounds too good to be true, but when you are living the Spirit-filled life, you find a lot of that. Let's look at these things one by one.

The Gospel is good news; that is the root meaning of the word. And good news is meant to be told. You may take your bad news to someone else in order to get sympathy, or you can sit in a corner and commiserate with yourself. Not so with good news; you simply can't exult alone. You've got to share it with someone, even if it means striking up a conversation with a perfect stranger. When your whole life has been changed by the power and love of Jesus Christ, when He's brought you out of bondage into liberty, then you can't keep this to yourself; you've just got to tell it.

During the period in which this book was in preparation, I had the good fortune to be invited to speak in Alaska. This was great good news for me, because I had always wanted to go there and had never had the opportunity. I found myself eager to share this good news with everyone I could. I managed to work the words "Anchorage" and "Fairbanks" into my conversations so that I could share with people the news that I was actually going there. If we are really rejoicing in our salvation, we will want to share the good news that we are going to heaven. If we are truly seeing God at work in our lives, we will want to tell others about the things that happen.

The perfect stranger really doesn't want to hear your good news or your bad news, because it means nothing to him; but the good news of the Gospel applies to him too. Sometimes this kind of good news answers a hunger that he has deep within him. Perhaps he is already a Christian, in which case your good news will remind him of his own good fortune, and he will enjoy having you share it with him.

Although everyone is not open to the good news of the Gospel, the Holy Spirit will lead you to the right people if you are open to His leading and ready to obey. There is a time to speak and a time to be silent, and this applies not only to occasions but to your relationship with people. Don't take your newfound treasures and cast them before people who are not ready to appreciate them, lest these things that are so precious to you be trampled in the dust. Seek God's guidance in this as in everything. This applies to those who are near and dear to you as well as to those outside your own circle. You will want to tell, but you must let God guide you as to who and when to tell.

How often I have seen people whom the Spirit has blessed, take their blessing and beat other folks over the head with it. Even if they are not self-righteous about it, they stand accused of self-righteousness because they are so insistent that others get the same blessing they have had. In England, I heard people handle this by saying, "I'm not better than, I'm better off." The comparison must always be of self with former self. Let your witness be a testimony to your joy, not your evaluation of the spiritual state of another.

What shall I say? In what form shall I cast my witness? How can I make them understand? Here we come to another basic principle of the Spirit-filled life. Let the Spirit Himself use your witness. He will go before, with, and after you. Before you begin to speak to someone to whom the Spirit has led you, He will already be preparing the ground. You don't have to work "cold turkey," as the salesman says.

I was asked to stop by a southern city in my travels and witness to a small group in the rectory living room. Among those present was a young Methodist minister and his wife. I was not aiming my talk at him, nor did I follow it up except to pray that God would use my witness that night. I remember that he stopped me at one point and said, "You are speaking of miracles, and I'm beginning to believe you. Do you know what that means? I'm going to have to reevaluate ninety percent of what I have just learned in the seminary." I heard later that he and his wife had both been baptized in the Spirit and that a real revival had begun in his church.

Secondly, as you speak, be very open to His guidance, and you will find yourself with an eloquence you didn't know you had. The Spirit will give you a freedom of speech that is wonderful to have, and if you put your trust in Him, you will say exactly what needs to be said.

Of course, I am a professional speaker, and it would be very easy to discount my testimony in this regard. But the audiences I address are far from uniform, and I find it as important to be Spirit-led as it is to be Spirit-filled. Coming to an audience cold, I find it quite necessary to be much in prayer that the Spirit will teach me what to say and when to be silent. When someone reports to me that I have said "just the right things," then I thank God for the guidance of His Spirit.

And thirdly, you don't have to worry about making them understand. That's not your responsibility. Simply be obedient: go where you are led to go, make your witness as you are led to make it, and then offer the whole thing up to God. This is one of the hardest lessons for us to learn, but it is a vital one. God can redeem our poorest effort; God can make of no effect those blunders of which we are ashamed. Those whose hearts the Holy Spirit has prepared will hear what God wants them to hear, and see in you that which God has made sweet and winning for them to see. And the seed, once planted, will grow under the nurturing of God if the heart is willing.

Experience tells us that the first weeks and months after receiving the Holy Spirit are the critical ones as far as witnessing is concerned. The biggest danger is that you'll get ahead of God, that you will not wait for guidance, and that your excitement over your new state will lead you to speak unwisely to the wrong persons. Take it easy. If you are asked to share with the members of the group in whose company you found your new life, you can feel quite free here. These are your friends; quite possibly they have already witnessed to you, and they are eager to hear about your newfound joys. But outside this fellowship, take care.

The devil walketh about like a roaring lion, seeking whom he may devour. He just loves newborn Christians. To eat up, that is. Put on the whole armor of God, and don't be rushing out to do battle in your own strength. The enemy will be quick to take advantage of that. You will find your witness rebuffed, your friends cool toward you; you will be brought down to earth very quickly by the power of the adversary unless you move completely in the power of God.

Of course, none of these dangers are before you unless you have so yielded yourself to Jesus Christ that you have been filled with His Spirit. He said, "Ye shall receive power," but only after the Holy Spirit comes upon you. Peter explained that the Spirit is given to those who take Jesus as their Lord and Savior. If you have not received Him in this way, do so now. If you have done so and fallen away, make a renewed commitment in this hour. And if you have accepted Him and been filled by His Spirit, then offer yourself as a witness, and you will be given an experience to bear witness to, an audience to which to witness, and the words with which to tell it all. You have everything to gain and nothing to lose — but your self.

# CHAPTER TWENTY-FIVE

## *MORE DEVIL*

Despite the lip service given to the idea in the creeds and liturgies of the great denominations, most people do not believe in a real and personal devil. Nor do they believe that Satan has evil spirits who do his bidding and who have their effect on the lives of people in this world. But Spirit-filled people believe this. They cannot help believing, because they have experienced the power of the enemy.

Whenever someone comes to the Church of the Holy Comforter in Miami to receive the Holy Spirit, to make a complete yielding of his life to Jesus Christ, we warn him to prepare for an attack by Satan. It is as if Satan is quite content to leave us alone as long as we do not try to draw too close to God. But when it appears that he is losing us, he takes action.

It is not good salesmanship to tell someone that if only he will give his life to God he will experience the power of the devil. But it is only fair to do so. It might seem better to do nothing than to get involved in a spiritual welfare, except for the fact that it is impossible to remain neutral. If you do nothing at all, Satan will have his way in the end, because by doing nothing you are saying no to God's call, refusing to acknowledge the claims and promises of Christ. Jesus said, "He who is not with me is against me." So you have to take sides. But once you stand up for what you believe, you have to stand up and fight.

The spiritual welfare that has been waged between the forces of good and evil is both cultural and personal. To look at our culture, our society, our age, would incline one to think that perhaps the forces of evil are winning. But study of other ages will show that the good guys have gained some ground. Reading the front pages of any newspaper will also show that the battle is far from over. Such a study makes you wonder what gets into people to make them do such things. Or we might ask *who* gets into them.

Spiritual welfare is above all personal. God has made you a person capable of great good and great evil. The choice is absolutely yours. There is a system of rewards and punishments for you as you go along the way. No one can make you do anything. God offers you promises and evidences of His goodness if only you will follow His way. At the same time, in immensely subtle ways, Satan counsels another path, while ridiculing and casting doubt upon divine suggestions.

What are Satan's methods? We have said that he is infinitely subtle, and such he truly is. Just as the disease of syphilis is called the great imitator because it masks itself as a dozen other diseases, so the wiles of Satan are such that one would never be aware of the source of his activities unless he was on guard and had the help of God.

Sometimes Satan will attack through physical sickness. We have seen people fall ill almost immediately after giving their lives to God. Surely a strange thing to happen. But it is not God's power that causes the illness, but Satan's. Quite often the sickness passes as quickly as it came, when the devil is rebuked.

A very commonly used weapon is doubt. He casts doubt on the reality of our experience with God, doubt as to the motives of the other persons involved, doubt as to our worthiness to participate, doubt as to the true value of giving all of yourself to God, etc. There is a vast difference between logical consideration of the merits of a situation and the kind of insidious doubt that Satan fosters. Prayer to God, despite such doubt, removes it quickly enough if it is of the devil.

But the deadliest of Satan's weapons is what I call, "The Sag." There may be a time each day when your strength runs out, and you just sag wherever you are. This is a physical matter, but it jeopardizes all that you are doing. In the spiritual realm, The Sag can come at any time in your spiritual progression. When it comes, you just go spiritually limp and feel like saying, "Oh well, I'm sure this is all very nice, but I'm just not going to think about it anymore. I'm tired of all this nonsense, and I'm going to do something else for a while." Beloved, such feelings, such thoughts, are not of God. Time and time again we find people who have once had a close relationship with God, but who have fallen away and have no idea of what happened. When you think of the joy and power and abundance of the Spirit-filled life, you wonder who would deliberately turn his back on it. The answer is that no one would, not deliberately. The craft and wiles of the enemy are such that with The Sag he can turn you away from the things of God without your ever being aware that he was the cause of it. If there was a dramatic scene with a big red devil with horns and a tail and a pitchfork who stood before you in a cloud of smoke and urged you to renounce God and come follow him, you could assume a heroic stance and tell him no. But he doesn't work that way, and it's ever necessary to be on guard.

Certainly, Satan will attack through other people. He uses them if they have no guard against him, and they seldom know they are being thus used. If they are not spiritual people, it is useless to suggest to them that their activities are being inspired of Satan. They will consider this merely a form of profanity.

Now, what can you do about these attacks of Satan? Well, first, you can put on the whole armor of God so that no attack can get through. St. Paul speaks of the shield of salvation, the breastplate of faith, etc. A heart that is filled with the Spirit of Christ has no room for any other spirit. But since none of us lives a sinless life, we are not always Spirit-filled. Dwight L. Moody is quoted as saying, "Of course I'm Spirit-filled, but you see, I leak." Therefore, Satan will have opportunities.

Any moment of weakness, of spiritual degradation, gives him the chance he seeks to attack. Sometimes sickness or physical shock sees the enemy creeping in on one who is preoccupied on another front. Grief or other great emotional preoccupation is an opportunity for Satan. And of course those who do not believe that there are spiritual beings — angels, demons, etc. — often expose themselves when half in jest they seek to conjure up beings from another world through seances, Ouija boards, and suchlike. They have more success than they realize. The experience of modern people, trained to think carefully and rationally, has shown a definite relationship between these adventures with the occult and resultant encounters with Satan's power. If you seek information or power from a source other than God, there is a terrible price to be paid.

So you can put on the whole armor of God, and you can guard against those opportunities to break your spiritual fortress that mental and physical preoccupation provide. But once Satan has attacked, once he has the tiniest foothold, then you must overthrow him in the power of God. And you have this power if you have yielded your life to God through Jesus Christ. Jesus promised that in His Name you could cast out demons. And you can. You have authority, and it takes no more than a simple statement of this authority in most cases. "In the name of Jesus, I command you to come out," or "to be gone," or "to let me alone," or whatever is appropriate.

If you take your spiritual exercises regularly, if you are in good condition spiritually, such exorcism works very quickly and effectively. If you are not in good condition, if you do not, from the bottom of your heart, wish to be yielded to God and not in any way at all to the things of Satan, then you may need help. Another Christian can pray with and for you and help your unbelief. Do not neglect to seek such help, but do not forget that God is faithful and loving and makes full allowance for the fix the power of Satan has got you in. God will make up for the faith you lack if your motives are pure.

I am frequently asked about exorcism for others. When we believe that Satan is influencing the actions of another person, we can pray for that person, and I believe God will make an opportunity for them to reject the power of Satan. But there's a matter of free will here, which indicates that we cannot cast anything out of another person unless that person is quite willing for us to do this. This is unfortunate, but true. I would also point out that in my experience, people who have just come to realize the presence of evil spirits in the world are prone to blame everything on them. Sometimes its just their own cussedness. They don't need Satanic inspiration to be ornery.

You can see that a dawning consciousness of the presence in this modern world of the devil and all his angels opens up a whole new realm of inquiry. It is too bad that most people get rid of superstition by getting rid of the supernatural, because the supernatural includes God and His angels as well as the fallen ones. This is not a topic which you can discuss at most cocktail parties. Many people will react with either laughter or pity for your ignorance, even though they go to church on Sunday and pray "to be delivered from the devil and all his works." The devil has very effectively gone underground, and if you begin to recognize his agents, you are one of a fairly select company who can do so.

I would counsel you not to become morbid about this part of your newfound life with God. Satan's power is limited to the power of suggestion. God can protect you from Satan, just as He can protect you from every other evil. There are unscrupulous "deliverers" abroad, just as there are "healers" whose ministry is aimed more at feathering their own nests than at glorifying the Lord Christ. Remember that Satan's power was vanquished by Christ on the cross. His shed blood is protection to whoever claims it. Put your trust in Him, and be aware and ready to combat spiritual danger wherever you find it. There is much to learn and much to do now that you know there is a war going on, but you are well armored and superbly equipped to do battle in the power of Christ's indwelling Spirit.

# CHAPTER TWENTY-SIX

## *MORE CLEANSING*

There's a little gospel chorus that proclaims, "My God can do anything." And one of the things He can do is clean up my life. I seem to be quite incapable of doing this properly by myself.

Now this doesn't mean that I am a weak person, without any discipline at all. It simply means that I am subject to all the temptations to which the flesh is heir, just like anyone else. And while I'm concentrating on one fault, another gets the better of me. Just when I'm beginning to feel a bit smug about the improvement in my sanctity, I find that this very smugness is spiritual pride. And while I'm working on that, something else goes out of whack.

I suppose you could divide mankind into two types of people, the disciplined and the undisciplined. I fall rather into the latter category. I'd like to keep a firm hold on my emotions, my appetites, and my habits at all times. But I love this life, and I love the people around me, and I wake up periodically to find that I've forgotten all about my discipline again and have just been living.

I suspect that I have a good deal of company in this category. People are not fond of discipline, particularly of discipline they have to impose on themselves. The church has two seasons in the year, Advent and Lent, in which she calls on her folk to take stock of their spiritual situation and to make some good resolutions about the future. In the secular world, we have the phenomenon known as the New Year's resolution, famed for the short life it enjoys in practice. And of course, one of the main thrusts of Christianity is the second chance. You can repent of your past life and start over again as many times as you need to.

But this can be a good bit like the fellow who said, "I know all about giving up smoking – I've quit hundreds of times." Repentant thoughts, self-examination, good resolutions – these things by themselves are not enough if there is no power to carry them out.

I want to suggest to you that there is another way. We don't much want to think about cleaning up our lives anyway, but when we do get down to this necessary task, we'd certainly like to feel that something more effective than what we've known in the past is available. And there is such a thing. Let me tell you about it.

In the first place, if you'll think about it, most of us are trying to change our lives without Christ. "Oh, no," you say. "He's the very reason I'm trying to change." But you see, Jesus has to be more than a reason. There are lots of good human reasons for living a different life, and if you are man enough to live up to what is expected of you in your own strength, then you can become your own god and turn to your own inner strength anytime there's something to be done. You meet people like this once in a while; they are not very comfortable people to be around.

The next thing we try to do is to study the Bible and the teachings of great religious leaders to determine what our course of conduct and habits of life should be. Then we draw up our own code of living; it may be entirely personal, or we may join a convent or a monastery and obligate ourselves to live by a rule of life imposed on all the community.

This approach is based on conformity. If you like a play on words, you can say that for some, the sacrament of confirmation is really a ceremony of conformation. You go to classes and learn what the church teaches about how man is to live. Then you go to church one Sunday and the bishop comes, and you promise to live that way for the rest of your life. I think you can find many people in the churches who believe that as long as they show up in church on Sunday, give some of their money toward its support, and do a little something about taking part in its work, they are Christians.

Well, let me tell you that I once belonged to a yacht club which had regular meetings that members were expected to attend. We were given quite instructive lectures on various things nautical. We were expected to pay our dues to the club regularly. And there were occasions of fellowship when we gathered together as fellow members of the club. But all of this had practically nothing to do with what went on when you went out in the basin, got in your boat, and started sailing. Being an excellent club member did not make you a good sailor at all. Perhaps the analogy need not be underscored. There are church members whose weekday conduct does not seem Christian at all, despite what they do so well and regularly on Sunday.

St. Paul says, "Be ye not conformed, but be ye transformed." Christianity asks radically more of us than that we join an organization, subscribe to a set of rules, and conform to a moral code. Christianity asks us to admit that we cannot make it in our own strength, to acknowledge that we need to be saved from a world that is too much for us, and to throw ourselves completely on God's mercy and accept His Son Jesus as our Savior and our Lord.

I'm very much afraid that a good many people are not looking for a Savior or a Lord. Their approach to Jesus is much more in the nature of a court presentation. They are trying to get themselves all cleaned up and dressed up by their own resources so that they can enter the Kingdom of Heaven proudly, as it were, and take their place as a saint among the saints.

Beloved, if you think you can make it on your own, you've got another think coming. When I consider how far I've got to go to be what God gave me the potential to be, the only way I can come into the presence of the Lord Jesus is crawling upon my knees. And I cry out to Him, "Save me Lord, for I am going to perish." And I am, too, if He doesn't do something about me. There's simply nothing that I can do.

When I call Jesus my Lord, I mean that He is just that. He is my liege, my ruler, my king. He has the power of life and death over me. He has only to withhold His hand, and within a few short years I will be nothing. He has only to withhold His present favor, and my life today will be a shadow of what it otherwise is. Everything that I have, all that I am or hope to be, is His. There is no other way.

I recognize that there are some who would meet Jesus as a fellow personage, who accord Him dignity as an honored adviser or consultant, but expect to have their own worth recognized in return. They are quite willing to hear what He has to say, and may follow His teaching if it suits their convenience. But to fall on their knees before Him and call Him Lord — this they do not understand.

We began by speaking of cleansing your life in order that it might be what it should be. Let's conclude by using this as one illustration of the way our relationship with Jesus works itself out.

If you could clean up your own life, we said, you wouldn't need Him. Yet many try it. Others join some group scheme of personal discipline. In both cases, there is this constant fretting away at our weaknesses, trying to hoist ourselves out of our difficulties by pulling at our own bootstraps.

When we turn it all over to Him, an amazing thing happens. When we give to God all that we are, both bad and good, His Holy Spirit enters our life, as it were, with a great big bar of yellow soap, and, oh, how He begins to scrub. Some of the things we had been worrying ourselves sick about, He ignores completely. And some of the things He begins to root out and clean up are things that we just hadn't given any attention to at all. Suddenly we find that we are new creatures, just as the Gospel promises, and that we are not at all the same persons we were just a short time before. The change has not come from without, but from within, where the Holy Spirit has been at work. We have not been *con*formed, but *trans*formed.

There is no rule in the charismatic movement against smoking. Hundreds of mainline churches provide ashtrays at their Holy Spirit meetings. Yet one by one the cigarettes seem to go out. Alcohol is taken from one and not from another as God works His will. Weight-reduction programs become a possibility even for the weak-willed. Honesty replaces dishonesty, openness takes the place of furtiveness, sexual aberrations suddenly come right.

Believe me, my friends, those about us will be aware of the difference. The whole world will know, sometimes even before we ourselves do. We will be conscious that people are reacting to us differently. That is because we are different people.

How simple it all is, actually, in the plans of our loving Father. Instead of this tiresome hacking away at one bothersome sin after another, we just turn the whole mess over to Him. We need only cry out, "Help me! I'm sinking under these many burdens," and suddenly we have a Savior, One Who comes to lift us up, to transform us, and to prepare us to live the abundant life which He has been promising us all along.

# CHAPTER TWENTY-SEVEN

## *READY, WILLING, AND ABLE*

The symbol of the Holy Spirit in the Christian church is the dove. This comes from the passage in Mark's Gospel concerning Jesus' baptism, where the Spirit descended upon Him in the form of a dove as He came up out of the water. I think we have sometimes been so concerned with His coming up out of the water, and the implications this has for baptism by immersion, that we have missed the significance of the coming of the Holy Spirit into Jesus' life.

If Jesus is God, why should the Holy Spirit come in His life? Is He not a member of the Holy Trinity fully equal to both Father and Holy Spirit? For that matter, we can ask why, if Jesus is God, does He pray to the Father? And the answers to these questions are of crucial importance to us as we seek to be Christians in a world removed by twenty centuries from this event at the Jordan River.

It is true that Jesus was God; Jesus is God. He is the same yesterday, today, and forever. But Jesus humbled himself when He came to earth. He became fully man while remaining fully God, but He accepted man's limitations.

In order to share fully what we experience, He accepted our weaknesses. He was tempted to sin, puzzled by the future, assailed by anxiety and frustration. If He had not shared these things. He could not be our perfect example, for we can see in what He did about our troubles, the answer to them.

In order to share fully what we can hope for, Jesus used, not His own power as a divine Son of God, but He opened His human life to be a channel for the inflowing power of the

Holy Spirit of God, just as we are able to do. When Jesus said to His disciples concerning His miracles, "greater things than these shall ye do," He meant exactly that.

Far too many people today set Jesus aside as a miracle man, one who came to earth with special powers and who could do great things because of these powers. The whole point is that these powers are available to all of God's children, and an important part of Jesus' mission was to show us how to use them. He did nothing more or less than we are expected to do and that we are able to do if we will follow His example.

Let's consider this under the headings of an often-used phrase, "ready, willing, and able." When there is something before us that needs taking care of, it is not enough to be any two of these things — we must be ready to do, willing to do, and able to do.

I suppose we all have the superman complex to some extent. Our childish dreams of doing great deeds never fade entirely away, for when they do, we begin very rapidly to die. Each of us has his favorite fantasy in which he or she is crowned Queen of the May, or rescues the imperiled maiden, or becomes King for a day, etc. Whether we are really ready to take advantage of opportunities when they come, is another matter. It is good to be a dreamer, but there must also be the readiness to translate these dreams into action when this becomes possible.

If we are willing, then we must also be ready and prepared. One of the marks of the Spirit-filled Christian, of one who has so yielded his life to Christ that the Spirit of God has come down on Him as He did on Jesus, is the willingness to go forth on any task that the Lord appoints. Such people make excellent church members because they are willing. This is one of the distinguishing marks of the Spirit-filled person.

Being willing calls for a measure of preparation that does not come magically upon our declaration of readiness. It calls for spiritual discipline and spiritual work; it calls for regular prayer and study of God's word; it calls for constant fellowship with others, constant sharing of what God is teaching about the work He wants done. Whenever I meet someone who says, "I used to have it but I lost it," I know that he has abandoned this threefold discipline of prayer, Bible reading, and fellowship. Restoring the discipline always restores the preparedness for one of Christ's faithful servants.

Now it is fair to say that when we are ready and willing to spend and be spent in God's service, God Himself makes us able. God is able to do exceeding abundantly, above all that we ask or think. And God gives to us spiritual power beyond the measure of anything that we can produce by ourselves.

For those who would witness, God provides the event about which to witness, the person to whom to witness, and the courage and the words with which to witness. For those who would counsel, God gives a wisdom far beyond the native capabilities of the counselor. For those who are problem solvers, God gives a perspective that allows them to function calmly under stress, and an insight into His will that puts them on the right pathway.

Jesus promised His disciples that they would receive power after the Holy Spirit came upon them. This power is still given. Trying to be a Christian without it, is like trying to drive a car without gasoline, or fly a plane without an engine. I have seen hundreds of average lukewarm church members become vibrant, radiant, and powerful Christians when they were filled with the Holy Spirit.

For those whose problems are within themselves, the very surrender to God's will which opens one to be indwelt by the Spirit, lifts the burden of fighting a battle in which you are both friend and enemy. It is much like awaking in the night and saying to oneself, "I *must* hurry and get back to sleep, for I have a big day tomorrow." There is no more certain path to insomnia. But if one thanks God for the moment of wakefulness, and begins to praise and thank Him for His blessings, it is only a moment until the morning when you awake rested and refreshed.

The Spirit descended on the Son as He came up from His baptism in Jordan. Before that time, He did little of which any record remains. But after the Spirit came upon Him, He was ready, He was willing, and He was able, in exactly the same way that you and I can be able as soon as we receive the gift of the Spirit which our Father holds out to each one of us.

# CHAPTER TWENTY-EIGHT

## *MORE THINGS*

I wouldn't go so far as to say that there is a good deal of the ascetic in most Christians, because I don't believe it; but I do notice that most Christians seem to think their religion teaches that there is some sort of stigma about the acquisition and ownership of material things. The church doesn't teach this at all.

The Bible says that the love of money is the root of all evil. It has nothing against money itself; it is a most useful commodity, and churches would be in a sorry state without it. But the love of money, the giving of one's allegiance to material things – this brings about evil results. Let's have this distinction clearly in mind as we think together for a few moments about the fact that for a Spirit-filled Christian, there are more things, more material blessings.

There is one more word of caution with which I would hedge this subject, and that is that no one should be encouraged to yield his life to God in order to grow rich in this world's goods. I suppose that is a proper motive for one who wants to sell his soul to the devil, but it doesn't get votes on our side of the fence. Our yielding to God through Christ ought to be motivated by a desire to become what God created us to be, to find the fulfillment in Him that is the natural goal for any man who can lift his eyes beyond the immediate demands of his sensual self.

When Jesus fed the five thousand, He was doing more than demonstrating His concern for the needs of those who came to hear His message. He was providing food for the hungry because God really cares about our material and bodily hungers. More than this, these miraculous feedings showed that if you give your attention to the things of the Spirit, God will take care of the things of the body, providing you use the good sense He gave you.

Any clergyman can testify to the truth of this principle. We leave the business world and turn our attention to things of the Spirit, and God takes care of us. That He does this through human beings who have to be reminded from time to time of the part God expects them to play, is only a natural facet of the human scene. I've seen a good many threadbare clergymen, but I've never heard of one starving to death. And while it used to be fashionable to keep our clergy in a state of genteel poverty, I notice today that the Lord is providing for their material needs and wants in an increasingly generous fashion through their congregations.

When my son Ross was fifteen, I had to explain to him one day that we weren't rich. He really thought we were. We had a swimming pool, a cruising sailboat, two nice cars, and lived in a good neighborhood. We didn't have a lot of money, but we had sought first the kingdom of heaven and the "things" certainly had been added unto us by generous parishioners and by circumstances. Further countering the worldly concept of apostolic poverty for the clergy, is the car I drive. In our society, we like to employ a lawyer who drives an expensive car because we feel that indicates he is a good lawyer. In like manner, a successful surgeon may drive a fine car as an evidence that his skill has been materially rewarded. But if we see a clergyman driving a Cadillac, we feel he is either being overpaid or is trying to be ostentatious. Nonsense! I have always enjoyed heavy cars, and now that Mrs. Hall and I travel so much, we do so in a Cadillac. It's not new, and it cost no more than a somewhat younger small car, but it carries us and our half-ton of books down the interstate highways smoothly and quietly. Thanks be to God.

But what will speak to you more tellingly than this example of a clergyman's blessings is what God does in the lives of laymen who dedicate themselves to Him. I don't think it's any accident that the revival of religion among lay people today is including so many who are comparatively rich in this world's goods. I think it's more than coincidence that so many tithers today are successful business people. I can think of no more telling argument for tithing or proportional giving than that given by prosperous laymen who tell what happened when they took Jesus Christ as their business partner.

Two things happen to your abilities when you yield your life to God through Christ. One thing is that living in Christ frees you to be yourself, to get the most out of your potentialities. None of us operate at full efficiency, because of various hang-ups that we have. Anxiety, doubt, fear, complexes — these things rob us of our greatest possibilities and pull us down. The Christian is set free from these chains, and can live victoriously in the midst of his problems. He is a much more effective person in every way.

A friend of mine is about to become a very rich man. He is an able businessman, but since he gave his life completely to Christ, he functions so much more effectively that he has been made president of several companies. Unless something goes very wrong, he will find himself a multimillionaire in his mid-forties. The fact that he believes this money will come to him for God's purposes rather than for himself makes him better able to earn it.

The other thing that happens when you yield completely to Jesus Christ is that with God as your partner in material matters, material things begin to change. The phrase, "you can't outgive God," is usually applied to one's church pledge or gift. And it means that the more you take God and His Church into your budget, the more that budget will prosper. This statement isn't based on superstitition, but on fact. Person after person will testify that when God becomes a part of their business life, little extras begin to crop up in every enterprise in which they engage.

One of our church members had stuck it out in a business that had gone bankrupt and had paid off every debt. He stood up in church one day and testified that he had tithed on an expected income of $12,000 the previous year and had made $30,000. He said with a little laugh that he was afraid not to tithe on the $30,000. The size of his tithe today indicates that God is increasingly blessing the partnership this man has with Him.

No one says that Christians lack for problems, but our ability as problem solvers is superior to our earlier ability, and we constantly find these little "extras" in the situation, for which we can thank our Heavenly Father. I believe a Christian should thank God for every material blessing he has. He should never feel guilty about his good fortune, because it is not fortune at all, but the gift of God. A Christian should expect to prosper in the material world, not because he is worthy, but because he is living an abundant life — why shouldn't he have some abundance?

Too many Christians are quick to complain that they don't "deserve" misfortune when it comes along. Personally, I hope God doesn't start at this late date to treat us as we "deserve" to be treated. If we are honest with ourselves, I think we will admit we'd be in pretty sad shape.

No, where material things are concerned, our prosperity, or lack of it, is more intimately connected with our level of commitment than with our moral worth. We don't deserve a thing from God; anything we receive, we receive because He loves us anyhow. Remember Jesus Christ, who died for us while we were yet sinners.

What does make the difference is our ability to function in God's world as superior human beings. Superior to what? you ask. Certainly not superior to another human; that's not for us to judge. No, we are superior to what we would otherwise be, if we were not living close to the heart of God.

This is the answer to the fellow who says he's just as good as the man who goes to church, or that he's doing all right now so why does he need God? Only God knows (quite literally) what can be done with that man's life if he lives up to his potential.

The important point here is that God gave us our potential. We can take no prideful credit for our talents; these are gifts. We are under an obligation to develop our talents, and if there is a proper kind of pride, it must have to do with our stewardship of what has been entrusted to us.

Only in cooperation with the Creator of this world, and the Giver of our particular talents, can we develop and grow and function as we ought. This is true in all the realms in which we have being — mental, spiritual, and physical. In the material world, the evidence is very plain when a life is fully committed. The abundant life is there for all to see — more abundance, and a more abundant use of what has already been given. Hence, whether it is loaves and fishes for our daily meals, or any other facet of our life in this world, I say to you, that with God, there's more.

# CHAPTER TWENTY-NINE

## *MORE HUMILITY*

There is something in human nature that rebels against the idea of being humble. To say that one of the gifts of the Holy Spirit is more humility does not offer a very attractive inducement to the average person. We want to be masters of our destiny, captains of our souls. Yet we have to make up our minds who is to be the captain, for it is only as we turn the control of our lives over to Jesus that we receive the Holy Spirit.

There are many ways of getting at the matter of original sin, and one way is to remind ourselves of our basic selfishness. Man is self-conscious: he knows that he is man; he knows that he is a self; and he looks at all the rest of the world from that vantage point. It is no wonder that he is self-ish, that he considers everything and everybody with relation to his own welfare. It is in our nature to go our own way, even when we know it conflicts with God's way. It is this basic characteristic in man that we call original sin.

But there is a thing called enlightened self-interest. This is the principle that governs man when he gives over some of his own freedom of choice because he thinks someone else's choices will turn out better for him. Thus a woman may abdicate some of her choices because she thinks her man can choose better for her, or vice versa. Thus we let a medical doctor make major decisions for us because of his skill and training.

It is possible to maintain that all decisions and all acts a man makes are basically selfish. The argument here is that man chooses and acts only within his freedom to do so. He may choose an unpleasant course of action, but does so because he regards it as the lesser of two evils. It can be maintained quite logically that even self-sacrifice is made only because such a course is most satisfying to the individual. If a man chooses to be self-sacrificing, to give his life to the service of others, it is because he chooses to do so for his own reasons, regardless of how unpleasant the resulting life may seem to be. This is not to be cynical about unselfish acts; we applaud them. But we can still understand that if the act is freely undertaken, then it is the choice of the individual which is being served.

To be humble is not the same thing as being humbled. The latter refers to something that happens beyond our range of choice, something which degrades and embarrasses us and lowers us in the eyes of the world. To be humble is not necessarily to take a lower place, but to take a proper place. Humility is not forced upon us, but is adopted by free choice. It is humiliating, as we use the word, to be forced by another to serve him. But it is not humiliating at all to choose to enter the service of another; it is an exciting and honorable vocation.

To put it another way, let us state that a humble person does not think of himself more highly than he ought to think. But by the same token, neither does he place himself lower than he should. It is only a truly humble person who is quite safe in discussing his own abilities with others, for he looks at them as they are in relation to the world, and not as he would pridefully like them to be for his own profit.

When members of a Spirit-filled group begin to share with one another, they can do so without false pride or false humility, because they are willing to face the truth about themselves. If God who sees them clearly can still love them, then they can love themselves.

The basic approach to humility then, is that one sees oneself from without rather than from within. It has been said that the salvation promised by Jesus Christ saves us from our selves. To become what God gave us the potential of being, we have to get outside of our own skin. The reason for this is simple. As long as we see ourselves, our abilities, and our problems solely from the inside, we can never see our situation as it really is. And no situation can be changed, no progress made, until one is ready to begin at the beginning, to start from where we really are. This is true realism.

If you have done much self-examination, you will know how hard it is to face things as they really are. The temptation is always there to make excuses, to pretend that things are not that way, but are different somehow. How can you build a life on such a foundation? With the power of God's Spirit, we are strengthened to look at ourselves in truth; the knowledge that He loves us as we are, helps us to love ourselves even in our weaknesses; and the knowledge that He forgives our sins, encourages us to admit them. How often in today's world do we refuse to accept responsibility for our own actions. We plead every possible excuse, from "the devil made me do it," to the force of the provocation or temptation that led us astray. Yet there is no growth until we are willing to start from where we are.

One aspect of humility is the acceptance of our true selves. The other aspect is the willful decision to accept assistance from outside ourselves in order to grow. Now this is quite different from using other people for your own ends. This is not humble, but rather self-centered. But to be willing to admit that others can do something better; to be willing to be guided by others; above all, to be willing to yield control, is the other aspect of humility.

Here we come to the explanation of the basic Christian paradox, "He who loses his life for my sake will find it." He who would have everything, must throw everything away. The power and goodness and love of God is far above anything that we ourselves can dream of being. If we are offered this power and love and goodness in return for abdicating our own self-supremacy, we would be foolish not to take it. To put it one way, by abdicating as men, we become supermen. To put it in theological terms, our highest destiny is to serve God and enjoy Him forever. To serve Him is to yield control of our lives to Him. To enjoy Him forever is for not us, but Christ, to live in our lives. This is not humiliation; this is fulfillment.

We must understand that our basic human selfishness is shortsighted. It would pull us down; it would prevent us from such a yielding; it would at the very least retain veto power on any decision or action that God requires of us. To reserve the right of final decision is to offer to cooperate but to refuse to yield. Cooperation is possible only between equals. To be humble is to know your place. To make yourself equal with God is a sin in the religious sense, but even for a secular person it is foolishness. Our personal integrity does not require us to be like the clay telling the potter what he can make of it.

The Bible makes many promises to those who will yield control, who will place their lives in the hands of the One Who created them, Who died for them, and Who longs to dwell within them. We are promised an abundant life; an eternal life; a life of joy and power; in short, a life containing everything that we cannot get by our own strength.

How does it work to be humble in our prideful society? It works very well indeed. The truly great are the truly humble. By great, I do not mean those with the ability to attract attention, but those with the ability to live in a worthwhile way far above the average. The truly great, the truly humble, have no illusions about their abilities or their weaknesses. They need not pretend nor worry about appearances. Theirs are yielded lives, and they are great because their cause is something bigger than themselves.

And oh, the heartaches we are saved by being humble! There's no more need to pretend, to put up a front, to worry about whether we are measuring up. We know ourselves, and we accept ourselves, and thus we can use our strengths and work on our weaknesses. Having yielded to the total guidance of God, we are splendidly led. Being empowered by God, we go forward in His strength. Being loved by God, we are able to encompass the world in our love. Truly, more humility is one of the greatest gifts of the Spirit.

# CHAPTER THIRTY

## *MORE SELF-ACCEPTANCE*

There's an old story about the traveler who stopped to ask a farmer in a field how to get to his destination. The farmer began several explanations of the right road, but each time he would stop and start over. Finally he said to the traveler, "Neighbor, you just can't get there from here. You'll have to start from somewhere else."

In reality, however, you can get to any place only by starting from where you are. The refusal to begin where people really are, causes tremendous difficulty in many areas of the life which we are living. You cannot start from anywhere else; you can start only from where you are.

If I want to learn a new language, it's no good my starting in the middle of the book, pretending to a knowledge that I do not have. I must begin at the beginning and master the basics, or I am lost. If I want to learn a new physical skill, I will only mess things up if I start banging around in the more advanced stages of the skill. I have to begin with fundamentals. If I wish to change my personality, it's no use pretending that I am someone I am not; in order to move at all, I must find out exactly who I am already, in order to have some foundation on which to build something better.

Some years ago, I become interested in amateur radio. Several of my friends were "hams," and I enjoyed watching them work their complicated apparatus, and talk to people all over the world. So I began to try to learn ham radio. Somehow, I just couldn't seem to get the hang of it. I came to resent some of the fellows who were less well educated than I, and who were not particularly sharp, but who understood electronic processes that I simply couldn't get through my head. Ultimately, I came to realize that I was refusing to start at the beginning. I wanted to talk as an equal with men who had been studying these matters for years. I signed up for a course which began with elementary electron flow, and soon I began to acquire the missing pieces of information that made understanding of more advanced theory possible. Not until I was willing to begin at the beginning could I advance at all.

Well, what does all this have to do with religion? It has a very great deal to do with it. Religion is our relationship with God, and what we do about it. Therefore, who and what I am is very important to the relationship. More than that, religion is going to help me develop into the person God created me to be. I am going to grow; I am going to move from where I am to something very much better. But in order to do this, I must start from where I am; I cannot start from somewhere else.

The trouble is that we proud humans don't want to admit that we are what we are. We go to great lengths, not only to wear a mask before others, but to fool ourselves as well. How many Americans wear clothing that flatters (and flattens) their figures rather than face the regimen of diet and exercise necessary for them really to look that way? How much easier it is to wear a loose-fitting sport shirt or blouse than to trim up what it conceals. From childhood we have covered our deficiencies with various fantasies, until now there is probably no human being living who is able to see himself exactly as he is.

Now of course, God does see us exactly as we are. Some people flee from any intimate confrontation with God precisely because they are not able to wear any masks with Him. And they don't want God to see them as they really are, lest somehow they might catch a glimpse of their own true selves reflected on the face of deity.

God is able to help us know the truth about ourselves. We don't have to pay a psychiatrist for this analysis, nor do we need to cajole our best friend into telling us. You see, it's not that the truth is hard to come by, it is that we don't want to know it.

While we were yet sinners, Christ died for us. It might be that for a really good man, someone would die. But Jesus died for us just as we are — poor, weak, deluded human beings. That death of long ago comes forward to this very hour in His present loving concern for us. He not only loved mankind that much back then, He loves me that much right this minute.

But if Jesus is God, if He really knows me through and through, how could He possibly love the kind of person that I know, deep down, that I am? I'm sure that anyone who could see beyond all my defenses would not find it humanly possible to love me. Ah, but Jesus is more than human! He's human enough to understand, but divine enough to accept what He sees.

Even so, I must run shuddering from what I see in His eyes unless somehow I can have His goodness and Godlike ability to love me in spite of my imperfections. And of course, that is what the indwelling presence of Christ's Holy Spirit does for me. As God Himself enters my life and transforms it into something more than human, the Spirit of Christ within me enables me to accept myself as I really am, to look at myself with all the masks set aside, all the pretences put down. And then I can shake my head over the mess that I am, but I can also get to work to become what God has for me to become, knowing exactly where I am and what I have to work with.

How many people do you know whom God has forgiven, but who have not forgiven themselves? How many people do you know who are unable to fulfill the commandment to love their neighbor as themselves because they do not love themselves at all? Oh, what an unhappy state! How many people do you know who cannot stand to be alone, who cannot stand to be in a quiet room, who do everything possible to avoid the moment when they must look within themselves? Beloved, the greatest salvation is to be saved from yourself. The truth, once accepted, can be dealt with. The truth, denied, will haunt your every waking moment.

The chains of sin need not be physical cravings or addictions that you cannot conquer. They can be no more than your refusal to face the sin. Until you admit the thing, you cannot get rid of it. When we speak of God whose service is perfect freedom, we mean the freedom that comes to one who has accepted Christ's acceptance of himself.

Jesus loves me, this I know, for His Spirit tells me so. I cannot live with Jesus in prayer and in worship without becoming conscious of His love. He knows my destiny, my potential; He knows what I can be; and if He can love me just as I am, then there must be hope for me. If He can believe in me, then I can believe in myself.

As a priest and a pastor, I know that a great many church members never go anything like this deep. I'm not sure whether some of them realize that they are fooling themselves. Surely they can't believe that they are fooling God. But so many go along with their little defenses, all their carefully contrived masks, hiding from the world the real self that is there. They play a part, and they play it so long and so consistently that they come to believe in the character they are portraying. Or at least they believe it most of the time. They shun those uncomfortable moments when it seems that the time for unmasking may have come.

Such people are never free. They deceive themselves as well as others. "Oh what a tangled web we weave when first we practice to deceive." Almost all of us are involved in this self-deception. How wonderful it is to meet a truly yielded Christian, one who has turned it all over to God, who has found in Christ Jesus the strength to accept himself as he really is. He is now able to relax in a glowing naturalness that makes him the envy of all.

Above all, those who let the Spirit of God indwell them so they can face the truth of their existence — these folk begin to grow. Some of the things that were once masks, now become reality. They don't have to pretend to like other people, for example, because now they really do. They have quit trying to get there from somewhere else, and are off and running from the place where they actually are. Now they are beginning to get ahead physically, morally, and mentally.

As long as you deny the disease, you'll never give the doctor a chance to cure it. As long as you deny the fact of sin in your life, you'll never cast it out. As long as you pretend to know more than you really do, you'll never learn. If you want to be what you were created to be, ask your Savior who has accepted you just as you are, to give you His Holy Spirit that you may accept yourself in the same way. Then a new life will begin.

# CHAPTER THIRTY-ONE

## *MORE TRUST*

One of the things I first noticed when I became converted and tried to give my life completely over to Jesus was that I no longer feared death. I am apprehensive about dying to some extent, as one might be about any new experience. I would want to die well, I wouldn't want it to hurt too much or be too messy — things like that. But the fact of death, what lies beyond the act of dying, is to me an entirely different thing than it once was.

I remember our Friday-night meetings at St. Luke's, Baton Rouge, when people of that city who had begun to be filled with the Spirit gathered in a circle to discuss the new happenings in their lives. One night someone said, "You know, I'm no longer afraid to die," and everybody gave a long and understanding "Yeah."

I have discussed this with other persons who have been filled with God's Holy Spirit, and they seem to know exactly what I mean. They have had a similar experience. In the first place, the Christian knows that death brings a fuller and richer experience of God, and having had a taste of such an experience in this life, he is quite ready to have it expanded when the time comes. In the second place, he trusts God to take care of him; he doesn't worry about it.

Let us distinguish between faith and trust at this point. Faith has to do with the probability of future happenings; trust has to do with your attitude toward them. We have faith that in Christ we have eternal life; we trust God this life will be without threat to us.

The opposite of faith is doubt. The opposite of trust is fear and the activity of fear, which is worry. Someone has said that worry is a circle of inefficient thought whirling about a central core of fear. Trust takes care of this by eradicating the central core of fear, and allowing our thoughts to proceed on a logical and less emotionally disturbed pathway.

I have referred already to my friend's expression, "Don't sweat the detail." Perspiration, of course, is one of the signs of extreme worry. What my friend means is that we ought to lift up each matter of importance to God, turn it all over to Him, receive His guidance and inspiration, and then go to work along the lines He gave us, not sweating or worrying about the details, but handling them one at a time as they come up, knowing that the entire larger matter is in the hands of God. That's one answer to the problem of worry — "Don't sweat the detail."

In this matter of trust, we must acknowledge that not everyone starts from the same point. There are individuals who are chronic worriers, and there are placid people whom nothing seems to upset. Some of this may be glandular, some may be due to environment, but whatever the cause, we are concerned here with the cure. Much has been written about fear, both from the psychological and the religious side. And it is obvious that whether you have few fears or many, it is possible to do something about them, to overcome them, to rise above them, to learn to live with them, whatever course you take.

One might think that courage is the opposite of fear. But as I understand courage, it is the willingness to go ahead in spite of fear. We do not speak of bravery except in fearful situations; the man who sees nothing to fear has no need of courage. Without question, courage is one of the highest qualities in men; it is a higher instinct which has enabled him to go forward when all his lower instincts cried out for him to do nothing or to flee. I suppose that as long as man adventures into the unknown, he will know fear, and he will need courage.

But let us be considerably more personal and private in

this discussion. It is one thing to face fear when you are part of a company of men preparing to storm an enemy position in time of war. It is another thing to sit half-naked in the sterile atmosphere of a medical clinic and to have had the doctor "break it to you gently." Or to see the figures which speak of financial disaster add up on a page, or to be told that someone near and dear to you is in trouble and beyond your reach, or to be guilty and see exposure coming. Most fear that we know is very personal, quite often inexplicable to others, and usually accompanied by a feeling of helplessness.

The opposite of fear is trust. Fear results from a threat to something we hold dear. Trust conquers fear by releasing that something to God. Now don't misunderstand. Trust is not the confidence that God is going to make everything all right, is going to do away with the threat and let you go on just as before. Trust is turning it over to God as a part of your total yielding to His ultimate will. What you desire so passionately may not come to pass; what you fear so desperately may very well take place. Let's be very sure that we are straight on this matter.

There are some who have no use for God if they can't use Him. In other words, their only motivation in allying themselves with God at all, lies in their desire to get the Big Guy on their side so that their side will win and they will get what they want. And when their side loses, these people are quick to turn angrily on God and His ministers, and accuse them of being worse than useless. And of course, if your theology is as childish as this, they are.

If you want the freedom from worry which is a part of the Spirit-filled life, you will have to relate to God in a more mature way than the person who is constantly running to the minister, asking him to get God to sponsor this or that project, or to destroy this or that threat to his planned existence. This is rather like the little boy who was saying his prayers and telling God he wanted this, that, and the other thing, until finally his mother interrupted and said, "Why don't you stop giving God orders, and simply report for duty?"

This is supposed to be one of the well-known benefits of a soldier's life, that he simply does his duty and leaves all the worries of existence to the higher-ups. Our relationship with God is not quite as simple as that, but it's closer to the soldier-service relationship than it is to the idea that some people have that God is sort of a pet genie that prayer lets out of the bottle.

Then, when you've got your perspective right, the next thing that helps you with fear and its attendant worry, is experience. You may not be able to see the silver lining in the particular cloud that's overshadowing you today. But if you have had a series of experiences with clouds, most of which turned out to be hiding quite wonderful outcomes when everything was said and done, then you'll face today's cloud with a quite different attitude. As you pile up experiences of God's goodness, you will find it easier, humanly speaking, to trust Him. If you will look at your own experience of persons, you will find souls there who have had much affliction and adversity on the human level, but who are not whiners. They "look on the bright side," because their considerable experience has shown them that there is a bright side.

Another human weakness that we must watch for in learning to trust God is our demand that He explain Himself to us. We are often so foolish as to demand that we be able to understand what God intends to do in a situation before we will yield it to Him. I don't know what you would call this, but it is not trust. If God loves us, if God is willing and able to take our lives into His keeping, then we must let Him do it on His terms, and we can do it in trust because He is the kind of God He is. We have not eaten of the fruit of the tree of knowledge to be able to understand all that goes on in the mind of God!

And so we come again to the matter of surrender, of yielding the totality of our being to God. We have spoken often in this book of the benefits we receive in the positive enhancement of our powers. But we cannot omit to speak here of the negative benefit we receive in being freed from the weakness of fear, and the nagging uselessness of worry, when we put the matter in His hands and say from the bottom of our hearts, "Do with this as seems best to You; for I entrust to You everything that is of importance to me. I know that You love me, and I trust You to deal with me out of that love." When the Spirit leads you into this attitude, you will find freedom from fear.

# CHAPTER THIRTY-TWO

## *AND SO*

I don't suppose you can have a summary in a book called *There's More.* In fact, the title ought to be written *There's More...* with three little dots signifying that the whole business never ends. This delightful occupation of discovering that the Lord is continually bringing us into new gifts and graces as we progress spiritually, is something that will probably keep us joyfully busy all through eternity.

If we haven't done anything else in this book, let us hope that we have gotten our eyes off of the one or two gifts or fruits of the Spirit that people get hung up on. By listing twenty-nine gifts, fruits, and marks of the Spirit, we are at least saying to those who feel you haven't got anything if you haven't got their particular blessing, that there's more to it than just that.

If you happen to be one of these good people, rejoice that God has more for you, and remember that He divides His gifts severally as He wills. He gives me what He wants me to have, what I need for the work He is calling me to do, and He gives you the portion that is just right for you. You can't really walk in my moccasins, nor I in yours.

There's a story about a man who fell down a well. No one knew he was there. He wasn't injured by the fall, nor was he about to drown, but he was trapped with no way of escape. So in his desperation he began to pray, and sure enough, the Lord sent someone to find him and pull him out. This so impressed the man with God's goodness, this was such a tremendous religious experience for him, that the next time he saw someone standing by a well, he pushed him in.

It is a human tendency to want to push everybody down our well. Not only do we feel that they would enjoy the same religious experience we had, but if we fell down the well headfirst, we insist that they go down the same way. We forget that God isn't bound by our rules, that He makes His own.

There's another story about a lady who received the baptism of the Holy Spirit. The way it came about, she sat down in her rocking chair, read from her Bible, and then began to sing a hymn, and the Lord blessed her immensely. So she ran to tell her friends, and nothing would do but they had to sit in her rocking chair, read from her Bible, and then sing that particular hymn. When nothing happened, they wondered if they'd got the order wrong — was it read from the Bible, then sing the hymn, or did you sit down first, and — oh yes, which way was the chair facing? We get so tied up in details that the Lord can't get to us. If we truly seek Him, the methodology will sort itself out.

We need to remind ourselves constantly to seek the Giver rather than the gifts. The key to this whole business is the yielding of self to God. When we get our eyes off Him and onto His gifts, then we are thinking of what we can do with these gifts, not what He can do through us. Someone has said that it is not so important to consider how much of the Holy Spirit you have, but how much of you the Holy Spirit has.

For those who are waiting around for the gifts to be delivered in a beautifully wrapped package, remember that they are yours only in process. The gift of healing is not yours to put on a shelf and admire. It is yours only in those moments when you are praying with someone and seeking to be a channel for God's power for their healing. Then the power flows. The same thing is true of all the other things God gives — they are given to be used in direct proportion as you let God use you. They are given that Jesus Christ may walk this land again in your body, seeing with your eyes, and speaking with your voice. You can be Christlike only in action, never in repose.

And so, if you haven't already begun, do so now. It's all there for you, a new life, an ever-changing life, an abundant and victorious life. And no matter how far you go, you'll never be bored, for believe me, there's more . . .

**COMPLETE NEW TESTAMENT KING JAMES VERSION
15 CASSETTES . . . $59.95**
**CASSETTE TAPES BELOW ARE $3.95 EACH**

**JB1 JAMES BJORNSTADT,** Author of "20th CENTURY PROPHECY"

**SBC RENEWAL IN SONG**—Sampler Psalms

**TA1 NICKY CRUZ,** Author of "RUN BABY RUN"

**TA2 (LTC) MERLIN CAROTHERS,** Author of "PRISON TO PRAISE"

**TA3 JAMIE BUCKINGHAM,** co-author of "RUN BABY RUN"

**TA4 ARTHUR KATZ,** Author of "BEN ISRAEL"

**TA5 DENNIS BENNETT,** Author of "NINE O'CLOCK IN THE MORNING"

**TA6 BOB BARTLETT,** Author of "THE SOUL PATROL"

**TA7 DR. RAY JARMAN,** Author of "THE GRACE AND THE GLORY OF GOD"

**TA8 MICHAEL HARPER,** Author of "WALK IN THE SPIRIT"

**TA9 BOB MUMFORD,** Author of "15 STEPS OUT"

**TA10 DR. HOBART FREEMAN,** Author of "ANGELS OF LIGHT?"

**TA11 DAVID duPLESSIS,** Author of "THE SPIRIT BADE ME GO"

**TA12 WENDELL WALLACE,** Author of "BORN TO BURN"

**TA13 DR. HOWARD ERVIN,** Author of "THESE ARE NOT DRUNKEN"

**TA14 CLINTON WHITE,** Author of "FROM THE BELLY OF THE WHALE"

**TA15 DR. ROBERT FROST,** Author of "AGLOW WITH THE SPIRIT"

**TA16 DR. J. RODMAN WILLIAMS,** Author of "THE ERA OF THE SPIRIT"

**TA17 SONNY ARGUINZONI,** Author of "GOD'S JUNKIE"

TA18 KATHRYN KUHLMAN — "AN HOUR WITH KATHRYN KUHLMAN"

TA19 KEVIN RANAGHAN, Author of "CATHOLIC PENTECOSTALS"

TA20 CHARLES SIMPSON — "A SOUTHERN BAPTIST LOOKS AT PENTECOST"

TA21 WILLARD CANTELON — "THE NEW WORLD MONEY SYSTEM"

TA22 THE CHARISMATIC RENEWAL —Bredesen, Ervin, Evans, Brown, Roberts

TA23 FR. JOSEPH ORSINI, Author of "HEAR MY CONFESSION"

TA24 PHIL SAINT, Author of "AMAZING SAINTS"

TA25 PAT ROBERTSON, Author of "SHOUT IF FROM THE HOUSETOPS"

TA26 MALCOLM SMITH, Author of "TURN YOUR BACK ON THE PROBLEM"

TA27 FRANK FOGLIO, Author of "HEY, GOD!"

## RECORDS

MS120 AN HOUR WITH KATHRYN KUHLMAN $5.00

M7 NICKY CRUZ — 7" record $1.00

M13-72 NICKY CRUZ — 12" record $4.95

M125 NEW WORLD MONEY SYSTEM — Willard Cantelon $4.95

MS121 TAYLOR MADE CHARISMATIC MUSIC $4.95

order from your local bookstore
or W.B.S.
Box 292
Watchung, N.J. 07061

SUGGESTED INEXPENSIVE PAPERBACK BOOKS
WHEREVER PAPERBACKS ARE SOLD
OR USE ORDER FORM.

| | | |
|---|---|---|
| A NEW SONG—Boone | AA3 | $ .95 |
| AGLOW WITH THE SPIRIT—Frost | L326 | .95 |
| AMAZING SAINTS—Saint | L409 | 2.50 |
| AND FORBID NOT TO SPEAK—Ervin | L329 | .95 |
| AND SIGNS FOLLOWED—Price | P002 | 1.50 |
| ANGLES OF LIGHT?—Freeman | A506 | .95 |
| ANSWERS TO PRAISE—Carothers | L670 | 1.95 |
| ARMSTRONG ERROR—DeLoach | L317 | .95 |
| AS AT THE BEGINNING—Harper | L721 | .95 |
| BAPTISM IN THE SPIRIT—Schep | L343 | 1.50 |
| BAPTISM IN THE SPIRIT—BIBLICAL —Cockburn | 16F | .65 |
| BAPTISM OF FIRE—Harper | 8F | .60 |
| BAPTIZED IN ONE SPIRIT—Baker | 1F | .60 |
| BEN ISRAEL—Katz | A309 | .95 |
| BLACK TRACKS—Miles | A298 | .95 |
| BORN TO BURN—Wallace | A508 | .95 |
| CHALLENGING COUNTERFEIT—Gasson | L102 | .95 |
| COMING ALIVE—Buckingham | A501 | .95 |
| CONFESSIONS OF A HERETIC—Hunt | L31X | 2.50 |
| COUNSELOR TO COUNSELOR—Campbell | L335 | 1.50 |
| CRISIS AMERICA—Otis | AA1 | .95 |
| DAYSPRING—White | L334 | 1.95 |
| DISCOVERY (Booklet)—Frost | F71 | .50 |
| ERA OF THE SPIRIT—Williams | L322 | 1.95 |
| 15 STEPS OUT—Mumford | L106 | 1.50 |
| FROM THE BELLY OF THE WHALE—White | A318 | .95 |
| GATHERED FOR POWER—Pulkingham | AA4 | 2.50 |
| GOD BREAKS IN—Congdon | L313 | 1.95 |

| | | |
|---|---|---|
| GOD IS FOR THE EMOTIONALLY ILL —Guldseth | A507 | .95 |
| GOD'S GUERRILLAS—Wilson | A152 | .95 |
| GOD'S JUNKIE—Arguinzoni | A509 | .95 |
| GOD'S LIVING ROOM—Walker | A123 | .95 |
| GONE IS SHADOWS' CHILD—Foy | L337 | .95 |
| GRACE AND THE GLORY OF GOD —Benson/Jarman | L104 | .1.50 |
| HEALING ADVENTURE—White | L345 | 1.95 |
| HEALING LIGHT—Sanford | L726 | .95 |
| HEAR MY CONFESSION—Orsini | L341 | 1.00 |
| HEY GOD!—Foglio | P007 | 1.95 |
| HOLY SPIRIT AND YOU—Bennett | L324 | 2.50 |
| JESUS AND ISRAEL—Benson | A514 | .95 |
| JESUS PEOPLE ARE COMING—King | L340 | 1.95 |
| JESUS PEOPLE—Pederson | AA2 | .95 |
| LAYMAN'S GUIDE TO HOLY SPIRIT—Rea | L387 | 2.50 |
| LET THIS CHURCH DIE—Weaver | A520 | .95 |
| LIFE IN THE HOLY SPIRIT—Harper | 5F | .50 |
| LONELY NOW—Cruz | A510 | .95 |
| LORD OF THE VALLEYS—Bulle | L018 | 2.50 |
| LOST SHEPHERD—Sanford | L328 | .95 |
| MADE ALIVE—Price | P001 | 1.50 |
| MANIFEST VICTORY—Moseley | L724 | 2.50 |
| MIRACLES THROUGH PRAYER—Harrell | A518 | .95 |
| NICKY CRUZ GIVES THE FACTS ON DRUGS —Cruz | B70 | .50 |
| NINE O'CLOCK IN THE MORNING—Bennett | P555 | 2.50 |
| NONE CAN GUESS—Harper | L722 | 1.95 |
| OUT OF THIS WORLD—Fisher | A517 | .95 |
| OVERFLOWING LIFE—Frost | L327 | 1.75 |
| PATHWAY TO POWER—Davidson | L00X | 1.50 |
| PENTECOSTALS—Nichol | LH711 | 2.50 |
| PIONEERS OF REVIVAL—Clarke | L723 | .95 |

| | | |
|---|---|---|
| POWER IN PRAISE—Carothers | L342 | 1.95 |
| POWER FOR THE BODY—Harper | 4F | .85 |
| PREACHER WITH A BILLY CLUB—Asmuth | A209 | .95 |
| PRISON TO PRAISE—Carothers | A504 | .95 |
| PROPHECY A GIFT FOR THE BODY—Harper | 2F | .65 |
| PSEUDO CHRISTIANS—Jarman | A516 | .95 |
| REAL FAITH—Price | P000 | 1.50 |
| RUN BABY RUN—Cruz | L101 | .95 |
| RUN BABY RUN—Cruz (Comic Book) | | .20 |
| SATAN SELLERS—Warnke | L794 | 2.50 |
| SOUL PATROL—Bartlett | A500 | .95 |
| SPEAKING WITH GOD—Cantelon | L336 | .95 |
| SPIRIT BADE ME GO—DuPlessis | L325 | .95 |
| SPIRITUAL AND PHYSICAL HEALING —Price | P003 | 1.95 |
| SPIRITUAL WARFARE—Harper | A505 | .95 |
| STRONGER THAN PRISON WALLS —Wurmbrand | A956 | .95 |
| TAKE ANOTHER LOOK—Mumford | L338 | 2.50 |
| THERE'S MORE—Hall | L344 | 1.50 |
| THESE ARE NOT DRUNKEN—Ervin | L105 | 2.50 |
| THIS EARTH'S END—Benson | A513 | .95 |
| THIS WHICH YE SEE AND HEAR—Ervin | L728 | 1.95 |
| TONGUES UNDER FIRE—Lillie | 3F | .85 |
| TURN YOUR BACK ON THE PROBLEM —Smith | L034 | 1.95 |
| TWO WORLDS—Price | P004 | 1.95 |
| UNDERGROUND SAINTS—Wurmbrand | U-1 | .95 |
| WALK IN THE SPIRIT—Harper | L319 | .95 |
| WE'VE BEEN ROBBED—Meloon | L339 | 1.50 |
| YOU CAN KNOW GOD—Price | POO5 | .75 |
| YOUR NEW LOOK—Buckingham | A503 | .95 |

# FREE
# SAMPLE COPY
# OF

# Logos

## An International Charismatic Journal

Worldwide Coverage
Feature Articles
Book Reviews
Trends

**order blank on next page**

-------WHEREVER PAPERBACKS ARE SOLD OR USE THIS COUPON-------

WBS
Box 292, Plainfield, NJ 07061

## SEND INSPIRATIONAL BOOKS LISTED BELOW

| Title | Cat. No. | Price |
|-------|----------|-------|
|       |          |       |
|       |          |       |
|       |          |       |
|       |          |       |
|       |          |       |
|       |          |       |
|       |          |       |
|       |          |       |

☐ Send Complete Catalog

☐ Free Sample copy of the LOGOS Journal

☐ 1 year subscription LOGOS Journal $4.00. Make payment to WBS, Box 292, Plainfield, NJ 07061

Name _____

Street _____

City _____ State ____ Zip ____